William Lewis, Esquire

Enlightened Statesman, Profound Lawyer, and Useful Citizen

William Lewis, Esquire

Enlightened Statesman, Profound Lawyer, and Useful Citizen

Esther Ann McFarland

With

Mickey Herr

Published by:
Diane Publishing Company
PO Box 617
Darby, PA 19023-0617
www.dianepublishing.net

Designed by:
Julie Tipton

Cover Design by:
Pam Otto

Hardcover ISBN: 978-1-4578-3207-9
Paperback ISBN: 978-1-4578-3208-6

Printed in the United States of America

Portrait of William Lewis, by Garth C. Herrick, 2007, after a portrait by
Gilbert Stuart, painted in 1797/1798. Photo by Fred Pfaff, 2008

"long may the citizens of Pennsylvania hold his memory in reverence,
as an enlightened Statesman—a profound Lawyer—and a useful Citizen"

From a published obituary of William Lewis written by Major William Jackson, August 19, 1819

This Book is dedicated to my son,
George C. McFarland, Jr., a lawyer, and
my three grandchildren, Megan D. McFarland,
George C. McFarland, III, and Elizabeth Anne
(Bonnie) McFarland,
All Direct Descendants of William Lewis

Contents

Preface

William Lewis came of age in an extraordinary time and place in world history—Colonial Philadelphia. Americans came together in the "City of Brotherly Love" to debate and declare Independence, craft the Articles of Confederation, and create the Constitution of the United States of America. During the colonial, revolutionary, and early national periods, Philadelphia was the foremost city in government, law, industry, and commerce. The city was a magnet for individuals preeminent in the realms of science, medicine, literature, and art. Philadelphia's lifeblood was enriched by a variety of racial and ethnic elements that made it unlike any other city founded prior to the nineteenth century.[1] The various streams of immigration brought settlers from Sweden, England, Scotland, Wales, Holland, Germany, southern and eastern Europe, and Africa. Thus, what started out in the eighteenth century as the heart of the American Revolution and the birthplace of the new United States gradually grew into the metropolis of a pioneering industrial and mining region. Those in charge had to both create and learn how to balance our national protective policy while simultaneously administering to emerging labor and social problems that grew out of a burgeoning economy. These changes in the trade and industry of the region were accompanied by equally radical inroads into the residents' daily lives, social customs, and mores, which, like the courts of law, and educational and religious institutions, were undergoing progressive modifications under the impact of all these new forces.[2] To live and work in Philadelphia was to live in a time and place where a person would have an impact.

The history of the city of Philadelphia and its first families has always held intrigue for me, not just because of the particular events that transpired, but because my own family played an integral role. My Swedish ancestors owned part of the original land in what is now considered South Philadelphia and Center City—a significant portion of William Penn's original plan for a Greene Country Town.

i

My great-great-great-grandfather William Lewis was a prominent citizen of Philadelphia during the American Revolution and the early national days; he was a successful lawyer, avid Federalist, and dedicated abolitionist.

Locating the important records of William Lewis's life has been a passion of mine for over forty years. Even in his own time, Lewis was noted to be "negligent of his papers . . . and cleanliness of his office."[3] Some of his most important account books have yet to be located, but, luckily, the legacy of William Lewis did not fade into complete oblivion, due to the survival of his country home Summerville. Now called Historic Strawberry Mansion, Lewis's summer retreat has survived more than two hundred years of urban growth and renewal.

Shortly after his death, "The Memoirs of the Late William Lewis, Esq. of the Philadelphia Bar" appeared in the June 1820 edition of *Analectic Magazine*. It was later discovered that this article was based on a biography of Lewis written by William Primrose. Primrose's version, however, was not published until 1896, when it appeared in the *Pennsylvania Magazine of History and Biography*, the scholarly journal of the Historical Society of Pennsylvania. The Primrose biography as published in 1896 seems at first to be far removed from memory some seventy-seven years after Lewis's death; it was in fact written in 1819 or 1820 and seems to utilize information provided by Lewis's immediate family.

In 1859 Horace Binney wrote *The Leaders of the Old Bar of Philadelphia*, referring to the first bar after the Declaration of Independence. Originally intended and printed for private distribution, the pamphlet was favorably noticed in the English reviews and reprinted in the *Inquirer* in May of 1860. In Binney's opinion there were three men—William Lewis, Edward Tilghman, and Jared Ingersoll—who, after the Revolution, largely contributed to establishing the reputation of the bar in Philadelphia. Binney was personally acquainted with all three men. Having studied law under Ingersoll and been admitted to the Bar in 1800, Binney was a recognized leader in the field of law in his own right.

In 1856 David Paul Brown published the first volume of *The Forum; or Forty Years Full Practice at the Philadelphia Bar*, in which he included a biographical sketch of William Lewis. Brown's intent was to put down in writing the history of the Philadelphia bar for the benefit of future generations. Brown, a lawyer in his own right, knew Lewis from an early age, having watched him in court as a law student in the office of Lewis's good friend William Rawle. Brown, like Lewis, would also become a lawyer for the Pennsylvania Abolition Society.[4]

My personal association with Historic Strawberry Mansion began in 1964 when I joined the Committee of 1926, the organization charged with administering the house. In 1966 I became a lifetime member of the committee, and by 1971 I also became a member of the Board of Directors. Also in 1971, I served as the president of the Pennsylvania Society of New England Women—the group that administered the Judge Lewis Parlor inside Strawberry Mansion. During this time I started visiting the Philadelphia Parks Department, the Philadelphia City Archives, the Historical Society of Pennsylvania, the Library Company of Philadelphia, and all the other great Philadelphia institutions, tracking any and all information available to ensure that the Committee of 1926 was interpreting the history of Strawberry Mansion correctly. This pursuit was key in uncovering the story of my great-great-great grandfather, and, ironically, it also led me back to my Swedish ancestors.

While commissioning a copy of Gilbert Stuart's portrait of William Lewis for Historic Strawberry

Mansion, I became acquainted with the Lewis family of Wilkes-Barre, Pennsylvania—most especially Mrs. Helen Dana, who was also a great-great-great-granddaughter of William Lewis. In 1967, Mrs. Dana and I officially unveiled the Lewis portrait that hangs in Historic Strawberry Mansion today. Since that unveiling, I have had intermittent access to some of the Lewis estate papers, which have allowed me to see Lewis from a vantage point that few others can.

For those who might be interested in searching further and asking more questions, the following is what I know of the provenance of William Lewis's records and papers:

- The executors of Lewis's estate were William Rawle, his second wife Frances Durdin Lewis, and his son Josiah Lewis.

- Lewis's law library went to his grandson William Lewis (1801–1889, first son of Josiah) who lived with his family in Wilkes-Barre, Pennsylvania. He also received the Gilbert Stuart portrait of his grandfather after Frances Durdin Lewis (then of Sunbury, Pennsylvania) died. Her will stated: "William Lewis Esq. Grandson of my dear Mr. Lewis Esq. one hundred dollars, together with his Grand fathers likeness done by Stewart [sic], hoping that he will not part with it, but keep it through his life or give it to the academy of Fine arts in Philadelphia as it is an excellent likeness."

- Upon the death of William Lewis (the grandson) in May of 1889, the library and Stuart portrait were given to William's nephew George C. Lewis (son of Josiah Jr.) A note dated July 13, 1899, handwritten by G. C. Lewis and found in the family papers, states that he was in possession of additional papers given to Josiah Jr. pertaining to Lewis's estate upon the death of William Rawle.

- In January 1916, George Lewis gave his cousin Henry Lewis (of Monmouth Illinois, also a lawyer) Lewis's Record Book and other important legal records pertaining to Lewis's legal career. This transaction is documented in a series of letters I saw in the family papers and took copies of in the 1970s. Despite my efforts, I have never been able to locate these transferred items. I know how valuable Lewis's Record Book would be to current and future researchers. I question whether these particular records are still located in Monmouth, Illinois, or where they might be. My hope is that they were donated to a learned institution at some point and will eventually be located and available to future generations.

- In 1978, I thought I had a lead to those items located in Illinois when I received a phone call from a docent at Historic Strawberry Mansion, who had just given a tour to a Mrs. Mary Lewis Weinberg of Augusta, Illinois, and her son William W. Weinberg of Quincy, Illinois—who had identified themselves as descendants of William Lewis. I spoke with Mary Lewis Weinberg on the phone, asking her if she knew of any family documents from William Lewis. At the time she seemed unaware of a connection, so I sent her copies of the correspondence between George C. Lewis and his cousin Henry Lewis, hoping she'd be able to shed some light on the whereabouts of Lewis account books that had been given to Henry. Unfortunately this was a dead end, as I never heard back from Mrs. Weinberg.

- The papers maintained by George C. Lewis were given to his daughter, Mary Squires Lewis of 191 North Franklin Street, Wilkes-Barre, Pennsylvania. The first time I had access to any of the Lewis documents was at the home of Mary Squires Lewis. In an initial short visit I was able to transcribe documents that she had proudly displayed on her living room walls, such as Lewis's oath upon becoming judge of the District Court of Pennsylvania in July 1791, signed by James Wilson—and the related testimony for the same position signed by George Washington and Thomas Jefferson.

- When Mary Squires Lewis died, she left the Lewis papers to her niece Helen Deemer Dana. It was during this time that I was able to have greater access to the family papers—through long-weekend visits in Wilkes-Barre and later when Mrs. Dana and her husband relocated nearby in Delaware. Unfortunately, both Mrs. Dana and her husband died in the early 1990s. I presume the papers are with the Dana children, but as these individuals are scattered around the country, I have not had the opportunity to verify their whereabouts (or that of the papers).

My goal in writing this book was never a scholarly endeavor, but simply to gather together all the information I have collected on William Lewis over the years and present it as an enjoyable read. I hope visitors to Historic Strawberry Mansion will purchase a copy, as the proceeds will go directly to the administration and upkeep of the site. Additionally, I hope this book will pique the interest of some individual who might want to research these topics further. To that end, I have endowed a fellowship through the Historical Society of Pennsylvania, which, starting in the 2011–2012 academic year, will award one Esther Ann McFarland Fellowship in memory of Judge William Lewis for research on either seventeenth-century Pennsylvania, with a preference for research on New Sweden or on the influence of the early Swedish settlers on the development of Pennsylvania, or on African American history. This annual fellowship supports one month of residency in Philadelphia for advanced, postdoctoral, and dissertation research. More information is available online at www.hsp.org.

As for me, beyond this work, I have had the joy of traveling the world, including all seven continents, crossing the Polar Circle, and crossing the Antarctic Circle. At this time I am very happy to have finished this book on the life of my ancestor William Lewis, Esq.

Esther Ann McFarland
Haverford, Pennsylvania
August 2011

Lewis Ancestry
of Esther Ann McFarland

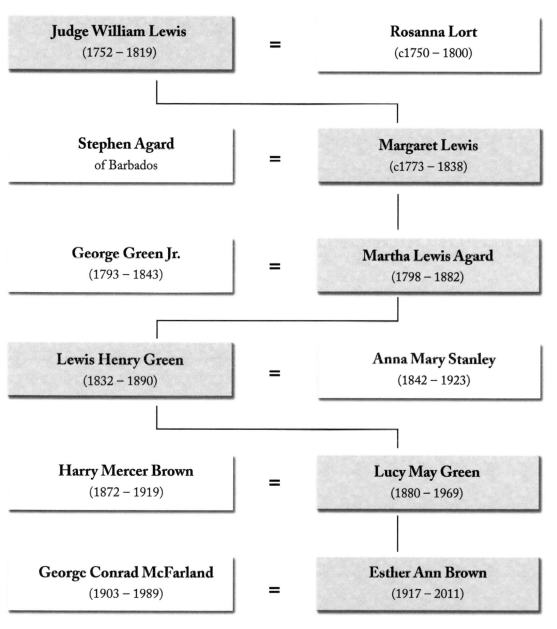

Judge William Lewis
(1752 – 1819)

=

Rosanna Lort
(c1750 – 1800)

Stephen Agard
of Barbados

=

Margaret Lewis
(c1773 – 1838)

George Green Jr.
(1793 – 1843)

=

Martha Lewis Agard
(1798 – 1882)

Lewis Henry Green
(1832 – 1890)

=

Anna Mary Stanley
(1842 – 1923)

Harry Mercer Brown
(1872 – 1919)

=

Lucy May Green
(1880 – 1969)

George Conrad McFarland
(1903 – 1989)

=

Esther Ann Brown
(1917 – 2011)

Credit Sandra Hewlett, Certified Genealogist

Acknowledgements

Esther Ann McFarland, sadly, died on September 20, 2011, before this book was published and before she could write her acknowledgements, which she saved for the last. I had the privilege of helping Mrs. McFarland write her book, so, appropriately, any list of acknowledgements must begin with her.

As a descendant of William Lewis, Mrs. McFarland took great interest in his life and many achievements. She was recognized as an authority on William Lewis. Indeed, Mrs. McFarland was made an Honorary Member of the Historical Society of the United States District Court for the Eastern District of Pennsylvania in a ceremony on June 25, 2008. Chief Judge the Honorable Harvey Bartle III spoke at the ceremony along with the Honorable Thomas N. O'Neill, Jr., Senior Judge; they agreed that "words are inadequate to convey the gratitude for her great commitment to preserving the legacy of William Lewis, First United States Attorney and Second Judge of the District Court of Pennsylvania."

Esther Ann McFarland, 2010. Photo by Fred Pfaff.

Throughout the many years that Mrs. McFarland spent researching and preparing to write this book, she consulted countless historians, archivists, preservationists—any person she thought might lead her to the answers she sought. She would certainly wish to acknowledge them all. Unfortunately, the names of many of those individuals have been lost with Mrs. McFarland. Those acknowledged in this list are the individuals who were involved in the last several years, the main time period when I personally became involved in this project.

First and foremost, we'd like to thank the Historical Society of Pennsylvania. Without the hard work and dedication of the staff at HSP and their care of the important documents and graphic images, this book certainly could not have been written. Special thanks go to Kim Sajet (President and CEO), Lee Arnold (Senior Director of the Library and Collections, who provided support on many levels, uncovering key documents, sharing resources, and serving as our unofficial encyclopedia of knowledge—thank you, thank you, thank you), Mary Grace Gilmore (Senior Director of Development), Matt Shoemaker (Director of Digital Collections and Systems, who also helped edit the maps included in this book), Tamara Gaskell (Historian and Director of Publications and Scholarly Programs), Dan Rolph (Historian and Head of Reference Services), and all the wonderful library and research staff through the years.

R. A. Friedman, whose initial involvement with this project started in the Rights and Reproductions department of HSP, helped locate many of the wonderful images used in the book and later digitized the images from family collections.

Jim Gigantino, Assistant Professor of Colonial and Revolutionary History and Slavery at the University of Arkansas, who spent time in Philadelphia in the summer of 2011 as the inaugural recipient of HSP's Esther Ann McFarland Fellowship in memory of Judge William Lewis, kindly provided further insight into the political climate surrounding the passing of the Act for the Gradual Abolition of Slavery.

David Maxey, who worked through the earliest draft of the manuscript and provided critical insight on the project overall and, especially, imparted his invaluable knowledge of the legal proceedings and legal records of the revolutionary and early national periods.

Theresa Stuhlman, Historic Preservation and Development Administrator, and Rob Armstrong, Historic Preservation Specialist, of the Fairmount Park Commission, helped with questions surrounding Historic Strawberry Mansion. Several who came before them helped solidify the provenance of the property, including former Park Historian John C. McIlhenny. It was great fun visiting Rob and discovering that the Strawberry Mansion files contained correspondence between Mrs. McFarland and Mr. McIlhenny from many years prior!

Sandra Hewlett, certified genealogist, provided research and insight into William Lewis's ancestry and important information about the many Lewis descendants. I know Mrs. McFarland would also like me to thank Sandi for her friendship and encouragement!

The hard working ladies of the Committee of 1926—both past and present—must be thanked for their role in preserving Historic Strawberry Mansion and telling the story of William Lewis. Particular thanks to current president Beth Kowalchick and the current vice president Melissa Trotter Horvat, as well as site manager Katy Beth Jerome, for their continued help and support. (Thanks, Katy Beth, for your last-minute research into Frances Durdin Lewis.)

Alan Kolc allowed us to use his wonderful photograph of the Strawberry Mansion gang, taken for the 2012 Academy Ball program—thank you.

A very special and loving thank you to Fred and Sandra Pfaff, Mrs. McFarland's longtime friends and cheerleaders of this book. As the unofficial McFarland family photographer, Fred took pictures at all the important occasions, several of which have been included in this book.

Many thanks go out to the various institutions that provided critical information and insight throughout the years Mrs. McFarland researched William Lewis and the story of Strawberry Mansion, including but not limited to: Chester County Historical Society, Haverford College Library, American Swedish Historical Society, Swedish Colonial Society, and Swarthmore College Friends Historical Library.

Thank you also to Dianna DiIllio and Victoria Leidner who helped with research, transcription work and some initial writing, and to the lovely Kim Schlicher, our devoted "reader" (who came into our lives at just the right time).

Rachel Moloshok—by day Assistant Editor and Scholarly Programs Associate at the Historical Society of Pennsylvania, by night and weekends our intrepid editor—provided patient advice and a ruthless eye, ensuring we produced the best book possible. She was exactly what we needed.

Thanks to Herman Baron at Diane Publishing for his honest insight and advice throughout the entire process.

And if these acknowledgements should start with Esther Ann McFarland, they should certainly end with her son, George, and his family. In Mrs. McFarland's last days she was mainly concerned with one thing . . . the completion of this book. I am thankful to George and his wife, Betsy, who gave Mrs. McFarland the assurances she needed that the story of William Lewis would not be lost. Thank you both for allowing me to finish what Mrs. McFarland started.

As this project comes to a close I find I am full of mixed emotions—at once overjoyed and profoundly sad. Working on this book after Mrs. McFarland's passing has allowed me to continue to spend time with her. I remember vividly the first time I met her at a party more than seven years ago. She was a petite lady with a big, loving, generous spirit . . . wearing a gold jacket covered with Noah's Ark animal appliqués. Our friendship grew through the years, and I am ever grateful to have spent such quality time with her in the last years of her life. She was a generous friend. I will certainly miss our afternoons at Grays Lane House, whether working away at her dining room table strewn with research papers or just having lunch at her little kitchen table.

And as this book goes into publication, I know she is here with us, clapping her hands and saying "happy days!" Because of her passion and resolve, the legacy of William Lewis lives on. Through this book, so does the legacy of Esther Ann McFarland. I am proud to have played a part.

Mickey Herr
January 2012

Foreword

As Esther Ann McFarland's only child, and co-executor of her estate, I have had the pleasure of helping to complete her book, posthumously, and having it published.

As the great-great-great-great grandson of William Lewis, Esquire, and especially as a former Philadelphia lawyer who tried various civil cases in the local courts—including the United States District Court for the Eastern District of Pennsylvania—I am proud of William Lewis's many contributions to the law, as well as his active role in the formative days of both the United States government and the Pennsylvania state government. He was indeed an "Enlightened statesman, profound lawyer, and useful citizen."

In many respects, William Lewis was the right man, in the right place, at the right time. All of this is detailed in the pages that follow, but here are some highlights:

Born in 1751, by the age of twenty-five he was already a leader of the Philadelphia bar at the start of the American Revolutionary War.

Given his well-recognized legal talents, William Lewis was called upon to take part in drafting the Act for the Gradual Abolition of Slavery, which was enacted into Pennsylvania law in March 1780. He would serve as a leading counselor to the Pennsylvania Abolition Society, where he worked closely with other PAS members—including its president Benjamin Franklin—litigating countless cases in an effort to win freedom for enslaved individuals.

At thirty-six years old, William Lewis was elected to the General Assembly of Pennsylvania in 1787, where he served until 1792. As a member of the Pennsylvania State convention, and more specifically, as a member of its ratification committee, he played a key role in helping Pennsylvania become the second state to ratify the United States Constitution in December 1787. Lewis also played a role in enacting the new Pennsylvania State Constitution in 1790, and as a legislator, he was involved in the formation of the University of Pennsylvania in 1791.

Upon becoming the nation's capitol in 1790—and hence the hub of law and commerce for the next ten years—Philadelphia's prominence in the nation's affairs put William Lewis, in the prime of his life, in the middle of it all. Just months after George Washington became President of the United States in April of 1789, he appointed William Lewis to serve as the first United States Attorney for the District of Pennsylvania, and later in 1791 he appointed Lewis (at the age of forty) to serve as the second judge of the District Court of Pennsylvania. President Washington's appointment read, in part: "Know ye, that reposing special trust and confidence in the wisdom, uprightness and learning of William Lewis of Pennsylvania, Esquire, I do appoint him Judge of the District Court." High praise indeed from our nation's first president!

It was not just President Washington who held William Lewis in high regard. Not surprisingly, on the February 7, 1791, Lewis became one of the earliest attorneys honored with admission as counselor to the bar of the United States Supreme Court. During Washington's tenure as President, William Lewis would also be called upon to provide advice and counsel to Alexander Hamilton, the first Secretary of Treasury, and Thomas Jefferson, the first Secretary of State.

Apart from possessing the respect and trust of our nation's founding fathers, William Lewis continued to play an important role in many high profile trials throughout the 1790s and 1800s. During the Revolution he had bravely built a successful reputation defending those accused of treason. This high regard would lead him to be hired as the defense counsel in a number of high-profile treason cases, including those that arose from the Whiskey Rebellion of 1794 and the Fries Rebellion of 1798. In 1807—despite his close relationship with Alexander Hamilton—he was called to serve on the defense team in the treason trial of Aaron Burr.

William Lewis, the noted statesman and attorney, was also a useful citizen. A founding trustee of the University of Pennsylvania, he would continue to serve as trustee for twenty-eight years. He was one of the original founders of the Law Library Company of the City of Philadelphia in 1802. And in 1805 he helped form the Pennsylvania Academy of Fine Arts.

Happily for me, he also found the time to marry and have three children. The Lewis family lived at "Fort Wilson" on the southwest corner of Third and Walnut Streets in Philadelphia, the former residence of Justice James Wilson (a signer of the Declaration of Independence). Lewis also enjoyed spending time at his country residence, "Summerville" (now known as Historic Strawberry Mansion in Philadelphia's Fairmount Park), on the banks of the Schuylkill River. It was there that he died in 1819, at the age of sixty-eight, following an illness. William Lewis was survived by his second wife, two of his three children, and thirteen grandchildren. It is through them and their progeny, as well as his exemplary legal career, that his legacy lives on.

George C. McFarland, Jr.
January 2012

The range of judicial questions which occurred between the peace of 1783, with Great Britain, and the end of the last Federal Administration of the Government, in the year 1801, the most brilliant part of Mr. Lewis's professional life, and when his intellectual powers were certainly in their zenith, was remarkably large and important. Before the country had attained the lawful age of man or woman, the fullest demands for juridical wisdom and experience were upon it. Questions of prize and of the jurisdiction of the admiralty—questions concerning the rights of ambassadors and the privileges of consuls,—concerning the obligations of neutrality, the right of expatriation, the right of naturalization by the States, the construction of the treaty of peace with Great Britain, the case of the Virginia debts, and of confiscations and attainders complete or incomplete before the peace, the constitutional powers of the Federal Courts, the powers of Congress, the constitutionality of the carriage tax, the nature and characteristics of direct taxes imposed under the Federal Constitution,—questions of conflict between the authority of the States and of the United States, and between the States severally under the Confederation, and cases of high crimes, both at sea and on land, against the United States, were rising up from day to day for solution; and in most of them Mr. Lewis took a part, and held a position, that was worthy of the questions, and worthy of his own powers also.

Horace Binney, *Leaders of the Old Bar of Philadelphia*, 1859

One

Early Influences:

A Welsh Quaker Becomes a Lawyer and Family Man

While one of William Lewis's Philadelphia contemporaries might have dismissed his rural roots and education, the Lewis family enjoyed a proud Welsh Quaker heritage. Lewis represented the fourth generation of his family living in Pennsylvania. His great-grandfather Ralph Lewis had arrived in Merion in September 1683 with his wife, Mary, and their children. Traveling aboard the ship *Morning Star*, the Lewis family came from the parish of Eglwysilan by way of Glamorganshire, Wales, after being courted by William Penn to become part of his "Holy Experiment." Ralph Lewis was one of six investors under the John Bevan Patent, through which he purchased 260 acres from William Penn in 1681.[5] Lewis's property is clearly labeled on Thomas Holme's 1687 survey of the area, published as *A Mapp of Ye Improved Part of Pennsylvania in America, Divided into Countyes, Townships and Lotts*.

The Welsh Quakers were most happy to hear of Penn's plan to create an asylum for the persecuted in the new world where they would be able to retain their religion, their language, and their honor. The Quakers had suffered especially after the restoration of the Stuart monarchy, as special

Early silhouette of William Lewis, with his signature (artist unknown). Society Portrait Collection, Historical Society of Pennsylvania.

1

Acts were passed preventing them from meeting and forcing them to take the Oath of Allegiance and Supremacy to the king and the pope. Those who dared to refuse could be condemned to death as traitors—the men drawn and quartered and the women burnt. Thomas Allen Glenn states in his book *Merion in the Welsh Tract* that the Welsh Quakers had few equals among the early Pennsylvania colonists in their education, industry, and practical ability. According to Glenn, "all their national pride and all their personal interests impelled them to undertake those enterprises from which their fellow settlers seemed to shrink. They were no pauper class subsisting or depending upon the charity of the Proprietor—but a body of self-reliant and resolute men with ample fortune in their hands, seeking, amid the primeval forest of Pennsylvania, a home of liberty, where undisturbed by priest or sheriff they could worship God after their own fashion. It has been remarked that of these . . . they were not only the first ministers, but the first statesmen, the first lawyers, and the first doctors of Pennsylvania."[6]

In April of 1701, to accommodate his expanding family, Ralph Lewis purchased three hundred acres of land from the estate of Barnabas Wilcox in neighboring Darby Township. This property, although not presently associated with the Lewis family, is open to the public and interpreted and maintained as the Pennsylvania Colonial Plantation at Ridley Creek State Park. Ralph eventually sold the land to his third son, Evan, in June of 1705. Evan, in turn, sold 250 acres to his brother Samuel—William's grandfather—for £60 in 1709. Samuel married a woman named Phoebe in 1712, and in March 1720 the two sold about eighty acres of their land to Joseph Pratt, then acquired another farm on Stackhouse Mill Road in nearby Edgmont, Chester County (present-day Delaware County)—including a farmhouse which also still stands today.[7] William's father, Josiah, was born the year prior to the move, but it was in this house that William Lewis, the second son of Josiah Lewis and Martha Allen, was born on February 13, 1751, as William's father had inherited the home from Samuel.[8] The property remained in the Lewis family name for well over one hundred years, until it was sold to William Smedley (related to the Lewis clan through marriage) in 1822.[9] The property, renamed "Raven Hill," has remained in the Smedley family ever since.

BIRTHPLACE OF WILLIAM LEWIS, 1751.

Etching of William Lewis's birthplace (artist unknown). From the author's collection

2

Lewis's childhood would have been typical of the time and place—filled with farm chores, religious meetings, play, and study. At an early age, Lewis was educated at the local school in Edgmont, but he was later sent to study at the school established by the Society of Friends at Willistown. According to William Primrose, the young pupil's progress was so rapid that he required further tuition so that his tutor could be fairly compensated for his efforts on Lewis's behalf.[10]

Lewis expressed a strong inclination for the profession of law at an early age. We have no way of knowing how old Lewis was when he discovered this passion, but several of Lewis's contemporaries wrote accounts of his visits to the county courthouse in Chester when he was a teenager. According to Peter Du Ponceau, Lewis was often sent to the city to deliver goods from the family farm to market. When he completed his tasks, he would visit the nearby courthouse to watch and listen as the lawyers pled their cases.[11] Primrose claims that Lewis was so enthralled by a particular trial that the family servant who accompanied him to market was unable to persuade him to leave the court after many hours. Lewis stayed until the court session ended late in the evening. Having lost his ride back, he walked home, arriving early the next morning. Du Ponceau suggests that it was after repeated visits that Lewis was struck with the idea that he could speak in the manner of the lawyers if he only had the requisite knowledge: "nature had endowed him with a clear, discriminating mind, a retentive memory, a powerful vocal organ, and an admirable fluency of speech. Nature had designed him for the legal profession. He felt the impulse; it was irresistible."[12]

Josiah and Martha were likely a bit reticent about their son's desire to study law. Certainly his mother would have felt concern about sending her son off to the city, and her Quaker values would have conflicted with the idea of her son leaving the family farm. Quakers in general were not much inclined toward courtroom battles and public conflict, especially if they thought such matters could be handled within the Friends meeting. But, by all accounts, it seems that his family supported him in his goals, making sure he had the right teachers and mentors and, ultimately, putting him on the road to success.

One such mentor might have been William's cousin Mordecai Lewis. A fellow Quaker and successful Philadelphia merchant, Mordecai owned a house at 336 Spruce Street.[13] He was a member of the firm Neave, Harman & Lewis, ship owners and importers. For a time Mordecai was also a partner with William Bingham in Mordecai Lewis & Co., which owned and operated seven ships in the East India trade. Mordecai's name appeared on much of the Continental currency issued by Congress in 1776. He would serve as a director of the Bank of North America, the Philadelphia Contributionship (an insurance company), and the Philadelphia Library, as well as treasurer of the Pennsylvania Hospital. Mordecai Lewis would have been a great source for William, contributing to his knowledge by introducing him to the arenas of finance and business.

Once in Philadelphia, Lewis was placed with Robert Proud, another notable Quaker, to learn Latin. Proud was the master of the Friends Public School in Philadelphia and would later publish the *History of Pennsylvania*—the first of its kind—in 1797. Lewis also attended school to learn German—a skill thought to be advantageous at a time when the German population was great and use of the language was especially plentiful in the county courts.

By his nineteenth birthday in 1770, William was placed in the law office of Nicholas Waln, an eminent Quaker and highly respected lawyer. He had entered Waln's office as an attendant more than as a regular student, but he applied any spare time to the zealous acquisition of knowledge of the law.[14]

In joining Waln's office, Lewis would have been placed among other students who had likely attended one of the Inns of Court in London, as was common practice at the time. Waln himself had enrolled in December 1763 at Middle Temple, specifically because he understood that studying in London was the best road to a successful Philadelphia law career.[15] Between 1760 and 1783, more than one hundred American lawyers received their training at the Inns of Court. This training was particularly valued in the middle colonies, and it had a definite impact on how Philadelphia lawyers conducted their business.[16] Later, during and after the Revolution, it became fashionable "to read the law" in the office of an established attorney. In this manner, a sort of apprenticeship system was developed wherein the practicing lawyer would instruct his "clerks" on the elements of law.

Having been the last student to enter the office and with comparatively less education, Lewis would have been judged less favorably than his peers, who, according to one account, took advantage of Lewis, subjecting him to menial services, errands, or whatever tasks they did not feel like doing.[17] On one occasion, Lewis fought back—not only did he refuse to fetch the water or deliver their letters, but he also lodged a formal complaint with Waln. According to David Paul Brown, Waln decided to "test them by the standard knowledge," declaring "that the man who knows *least*, should serve the others." After the examination, Waln found that Lewis was the most knowledgeable student in the office. His days of serving the other students were over. Another of Lewis's contemporaries, Horace Binney, observed, "He must have read law intensely at some period of his life, as no man of his day knew the doctrines of the common law better."[18] There would be ample opportunity to learn, as Waln was consulted by lawyers throughout the colonies. There was also ample opportunity to earn, as by the year 1771 Lewis's income was said to exceed £2,000 a year.

Lewis's focus on his professional life did not mean he put his personal life aside. He was not long in town before he met Rosanna Lort. Born about 1750, Rosanna was the daughter of John Lort and his second wife, Barbara Jones (Crozier). Rosanna had a half sister, Margaret, from her mother's first marriage to Mr. Crozier, and two younger brothers, John Jr. and Joseph.[19] Through her maternal line, Rosanna was descended from the Swedish settlers who predated William Penn's arrival by several generations and who were the first European owners of the land upon which Penn would build his new city. It was not uncommon for Quakers who lived and worked in Philadelphia during this era to marry outside the Society of Friends, as Lewis did. There is no record of how the Lewis family reacted or if they attended the ceremony, but on November 25, 1771, Rosanna and William were married at St. Michael's and Zion Evangelical Lutheran Church in Philadelphia. The records of the church state the following:

> By license dated November 25, 1771, William Lewis of Chester County, Gentl. And Rosanna Lort of Philadelphia spinster. Witnessed: her father And her sister.[20]

It was at this same time that Lewis's mentor Nicholas Waln was suffering a change of heart. He too had just been married. His new wife was Sarah Richardson, the only child of a wealthy Philadelphia merchant. Prior to his marriage, Waln was by all accounts considered prosperous, well dressed, and happiest when riding through town in his bright yellow carriage.[21] In the winter of 1771–1772, however, after winning a case for a client he thought guilty, it appears that Waln was overcome by a sense of remorse. So extraordinary was his guilt that when he attended a Society of Friends meeting in Philadelphia a few days later, his public prayer—a veritable outburst in a normally silent meeting—

was immediately recorded by several who heard it.[22] As he kneeled down and spoke, he acknowledged his sins and transgressions and stated that he would sacrifice his life to follow the Lord. He kept to his house for some weeks after, eventually closing down his law practice and taking on the dress and manner of a plain Quaker. He would thereafter dedicate the rest of his life to the work of the Society of Friends.

Waln's clients now faced the choice of requesting a refund for fees and engaging new counsel or leaving their concerns in the care of one of Waln's students. Although not yet a member of the bar, Lewis was so highly respected that those clients whose cases did not require a trial were happy to leave their business in his able hands.[23] By the age of twenty-two, Lewis already had a growing legal practice; he became a member of the Philadelphia Bar on September 4, 1773. In December of that year he was admitted to the Court of Common Pleas.

While Lewis was busy building his law practice, his wife was busy at home with their three children. Born in quick succession were a son, Josiah, in 1772, a daughter, Margaret, in 1773, and a second daughter, Martha, in 1774. His relative success, however, did not go unnoticed by the Society of Friends, which did not look kindly upon his choice of wife or of career. Like others of his time who chose contrary to their religious upbringing, Lewis was officially disowned by the Friends on October 25, 1775.[24] According to the records of the Monthly Meeting of Friends in Philadelphia, held at their meeting house on Pine Street, it was not just Lewis's marriage the Friends disliked, but his friends and associates as well. On February 21, 1776, the following testimony was read and agreed to:

> William Lewis of this City turner, who was educated and made Profession with us, by not attending to the Dictates of Truth in his own mind, hath indulg'd himself in keeping Unprofitable Company; having moreover accomplished his Marriage contrary to the rules of our Discipline; and hath also of late, so far deviated from our Peaceable Principles as to join with Others, in learning the Art of War. For all which he hath been tenderly treated with, in order to bring him to a du [sic] sense of his Misconduct; but our Labours of Love not having the desired effect: We testify, he hath thereby Disunited himself from Religious Fellowship with us, until he becomes sensible of his transgression, and also of his deviation from our Testimony & Discipline as before mention'd; and Condemns the same to the satisfaction of this Meeting which that he may (thro' a close Attention to the Dictates of Divine Grace) be enabled to do, is our desire.[25]

It doesn't appear that Lewis was much bothered by this testimony; the Monthly Meeting records indicate that he declined to appeal it.[26] He was twenty-five years old and focused on the future. By June of 1776 Lewis would lead the bar in the number of actions recorded in the Court of Common Pleas.[27] As it turned out, these actions would be the last entries of the last term of the Court of Common Pleas in Pennsylvania recorded on behalf of the British royal government. In a matter of weeks the American colonies would declare their independence from the British. Everything Lewis thought he knew was about to change. The city he loved and the neighborhood he lived in would soon become the epicenter of government, law, industry, and commerce for the next twenty-five years. A whole new world order would need to be created. William Lewis was ready for the challenge.

Two

Declaring Independence:

Lewis Builds his Legal Reputation in a Time of Turmoil

By declaring independence from the British, the American colonists had taken on the task of simultaneously crafting a new political philosophy and creating a new governmental structure. William Lewis, the plucky young man who joined the Philadelphia bar just three years prior to the start of the Revolution, was in an ideal position to become both a principal player and a major influence on the legal and constitutional developments of the burgeoning United States of America. Questions of loyalty, definitions of treason, considerations of individual rights and states' rights versus the rights of the emerging nation, and the challenges of ensuring a fair judiciary were all matters of importance to Lewis. By the time the framers of the Constitution sought to "establish Justice, insure domestic Tranquility, provide for the common defense, promote the general Welfare, and secure the Blessings of Liberty," Lewis would not only have built a strong opinion but would become a respected voice amid the debate on how such lofty goals might be accomplished.

In his prime, William Lewis evoked strong reactions from those who came in contact with him. Lewis stood six feet tall, although it is said he developed a bit of a stoop in later years. He had a large, prominent nose of which he was known to be quite proud. His disdain for all things French kept him in knee breeches and powdered wig long after the French Revolutionaries influenced his contemporaries to take up wearing pantaloons and discard their hairpieces. Lewis was an incessant smoker, preferring cigars above all else. One can easily envision the lanky Mr. Lewis as John Watson described him "on for a fine day in front of his office walking slowly up and down smoking his 'segar.'"[28] Robert Smith was apparently so taken by Lewis's characteristics that he was impelled to pick up a pen to get them down on paper while they sat at a meeting—the prominent nose, the ever-present cigar, and the spectacles pushed up onto his forehead.[29] Lewis's unique features were captured on several occasions. One image by Albert Rosenthal is based on the contemporaneous drawing by Smith. Another by David McNeilly Stauffer focuses on Lewis's nose and ubiquitous cigar.

Line drawing of William Lewis with a cigar, by David McNeilly Stauffer. Society Portrait Collection, Historical Society of Pennsylvania.

Portrait of William Lewis by Albert Rosenthal, from a contemporaneous drawing by Robert Smith. Society Portrait Collection, Historical Society of Pennsylvania.

Lewis's actions as a lawyer and legislator (and, later, as a United States District Court judge) were informed by the values he had learned as a child. His Quaker ancestors had come to the colonies to escape religious persecution. His family had worked diligently to create a society based on honor, respect, and fairness. Freedom from unjust punishment and the ability to have a trial by jury—as William Penn had envisioned—were principles of utmost importance to Lewis. Above all, he valued the rights of the individual. Eventually, Lewis would become a key player in the Federalist Party. He believed in the need for a fiscally sound and strong national government. These ideals would become the driving force in Lewis's passion for the law and legislature in the years to come.

It is said that Lewis's passion was most evident when he was observed "in action." David Paul Brown, who saw Lewis's performances in court on countless occasions, commented that witnessing Lewis in court for the first time "stirred men's blood, and caused the hair to stand on end."[30] Brown also noted Lewis's repeated use of a gesture he describes as "that of raising his right arm almost perpendicularly, and as though in the act of throwing a tomahawk, and sometimes bringing it down with great violence upon the desk."[31]

While these descriptions might sound a bit like a caricature, their effect in court seems to have come across as anything but—in person, it seems, what came through was Lewis's passion and knowledge. This was well illustrated in the summer of 1794 when a contingent of five Chickasaw chiefs—in town to gain the assurances of Washington that their territory would be protected by the United States—were asked their opinion of Lewis after seeing him speak before the court. [32] The Native American dignitaries, some in trousers and shirts in deference to the President, the others bare-chested, sporting silver breastplates, face paint, and nose rings, declared Lewis a "great warrior" even though they had a limited understanding of his speech.[33] They did not need to understand the words to understand the emotions behind them.

As he did before becoming a member of the Philadelphia Bar, Lewis continued to service his clients' administrative needs, such as securing payments of debts, processing insurance claims, and leasing real estate. Although Lewis's practice would continue to handle this type of work throughout his career, once the colonists declared their independence from the British, the breadth of his cases would take on many unexpected forms, and he would find himself immersed in issues he might not have ever imagined.

The Province of Pennsylvania was a proprietary colony granted to William Penn by King Charles II of England. At the time the representatives of the thirteen American colonies declared their independence, Pennsylvania's government was directed under a "Charter of Privileges" granted by William Penn in 1701. With the overthrow of British authority came the need for a new government. In a sense, everything was up for reinterpretation and re-creation.

The struggle for political power was great. An interim Council for Safety was created to manage any immediate concerns in Pennsylvania. The Council became the de facto governing body, superseding any prior authorities. For example, the mayor of Philadelphia, Samuel Powel, was dismissed from duty. William Lewis and his fellow lawyers became involved in a battle between the so-called Conservatives of Philadelphia—which included most of the city's attorneys—and the Radicals (also referred to as Constitutionalists) from the state's western counties. By September of 1776, representatives from throughout the state came together for the first state convention to discuss the significant issues. The meeting resulted in a new state constitution that provided an assembly of one House and a Supreme Executive Council instead of a governor. The Conservatives were not happy, as this new constitution—in their view—was too extreme in its democratic allowances. It had gone far beyond any actions taken by the other American colonies, and under it the Conservatives would lose much control. In an attempt to hinder the new government, most Conservatives refused to accept any posts offered to them by the new administration.[34] The Conservatives—Lewis foremost among them—immediately began agitating for a new constitutional convention. Nothing would proceed on this front for another eleven years.

In the meantime, during the first session held under the new authority of the Commonwealth in September 1777, six lawyers were admitted to Pennsylvania's Court of Common Pleas to resume their practice: John Morris, John Haley, William Lewis, Andrew Robeson, Jacob Rush, and Jonathan D. Sergeant.[35] Lewis was also admitted to the Supreme Court of Pennsylvania under Chief Justice McKean for the September 1777 term.[36] The courts in Philadelphia had barely gotten up and running when the British arrived in town. Jacob J. Hiltzheimer, a citizen of Philadelphia, was most succinct in his journal entry for that date: "September 26—This day the English entered Philadelphia."[37]

Many patriots, fearing for their lives and the safety of their families, hastily left town. William Lewis was forced to do likewise, moving his family to temporary quarters with his parents in Edgmont, Chester County. Lewis was able to continue practicing law once he took the Oath of Allegiance administered by Dan Griffith at the Chester County Court.[38] Lewis and his family would remain in Chester County for almost a year until the British forces pulled out of Philadelphia in mid-June 1778. The war was still in full progress, but a change in strategy caused the British to abandon their hold on Philadelphia and instead march toward New York.

Upon his return to Philadelphia, Lewis found a city full of fervor. The British left behind property damage and hard feelings. Once the patriots regained the city, Philadelphians who had remained during the occupation were suspected of disloyalty—especially those individuals who had profited from or aided the British in some manner. As early as July 17, just a few weeks after the British had gone, an association was formed to identify Tories (those loyal to the British). Within five weeks, proclamations attached the taint of treason to 139 persons, including shopkeepers, laborers, and artisans.[39] These individuals were often charged with treason by vigilante mobs intent on revenge. Further still, as Quakers did not believe in taking up arms, popular interest defined every Friend as a Tory.

Lewis was alarmed by this rush to judgment. Where in the actions of these vigilantes was a person's right to religious freedom or trial by jury? In July of 1778, Lewis pleaded with the Supreme Executive Council to issue a proclamation stating, "as the Civil Authority is now reestablished in this City, those who have offended against the Laws of the Land will be called to answer, and punished according to their Demerits; and therefore forbidding the taking of Private Revenge."[40] A guilty verdict for those accused of treason could very well mean death.

Beyond his plea to the Supreme Executive Council, Lewis went one step further when he became one of a very small number of lawyers willing to defend those charged with treason. He was particularly alarmed by accusations stemming from guilt by association and, of course, by the accusations lodged against those of the Quaker faith. He became their champion. Either Lewis or his fellow counselor and friend James Wilson—or both—appeared for the defense in nearly every treason case that was docketed in Pennsylvania through 1799.[41] In essence, over twenty-five years, Lewis did everything in his power to uphold the spirit of the law—to protect individual liberty—and to avoid the influence of popular pressure.

Two early cases of importance in 1778 involved Abraham Carlisle and John Roberts. The significance of these cases is that each of these accusations of treason appears to have been politically motivated. The Council wanted to show their toughness toward collaborators, and they were determined to set early and harsh examples in order to frighten Loyalists. In the Council's estimation, for someone to associate with the forces of the enemy in any way was a sufficiently overt act of levying war. Lewis and like-minded individuals hoped to show that the presence of noncombatants such as the Quakers made it essential to distinguish between "active adherence to the British cause and mere refusal to participate in matters of a military nature."[42] On September 25, 1778, Lewis—acting as the junior representative—along with co-counsel George Ross and James Wilson, argued three main points in *Respublica v. Carlisle*. First, they contended that there was no proof of overt act of treason (defined as furnishing the enemy with provisions, enlisting in their army, or engaging in traitorous correspondence with them). They pointed out, furthermore, that there had been no use of a weapon. Finally, they argued that during British occupation, the people of Philadelphia were no longer under the protection of the commonwealth but were citizens of a conquered city.[43]

Carlisle was an elderly, prosperous Philadelphia carpenter who had offered his services to the British as a guard at the city gates. For this action, he was found guilty of treason. His defense team appealed the case to the Pennsylvania Supreme Court. In addition, the Supreme Executive Council was petitioned on Carlisle's behalf, and several citizens sent written testimonials. These actions were all to no avail, as the appeals were turned down.

Five days later, on September 30, 1778, Lewis was once again on the defense—as junior counselor with Wilson and Ross—in the highly publicized case against John Roberts. Roberts was a miller, a third-generation American, and a Quaker from the Merion Friends Meeting. As such, he sided neither with the patriots nor the Tories. His neutral stance incurred threatening behavior from his neighbors, forcing him to flee to the city for protection during the British occupation. Before returning home, Roberts was ordered by the Supreme Executive Council to answer to charges of high treason; after doing so, he pledged his allegiance to Pennsylvania and America. He then returned to his home and large family in Lower Merion. Despite his pledge, he was arrested and sent back to the city to stand trial. Roberts was charged with "ridiculing the American cause, predicting the British would eventually vanquish the American rebellion and attempting to persuade individuals to enlist in the British army."[44] The jury ultimately found him guilty. Roberts's case was also appealed to the Pennsylvania Supreme Court, and he was once again found guilty as charged. Despite the verdict, some still believed the circumstances should have allowed for Roberts to be granted clemency. Both Carlisle and Roberts were hanged on November 4, 1778.

Overall, the 1778 Philadelphia term of the Pennsylvania Supreme Court held great opportunity for the Philadelphia lawyers, especially for talented young practitioners such as William Lewis. As historian Thomas Meehan observed, "with more clients than they could attend, with opportunity . . . for setting precedents in American law, [and] with the possibility of winning political as well as legal battles in court," Pennsylvania lawyers found the new court term irresistible.[45] It is during this period that Lewis started to grow into his full potential and to build his reputation. As the lawyer uniformly on the side of the defendant—especially in matters of treason—he became known for his passion, for his mastery of the details, and for the well-placed barbs at the tip of his tongue.[46]

Another one of Lewis's big cases in 1778 involved the capture of the sloop *Active*, which pitted the rights of our burgeoning nation against those of the state of Pennsylvania. According to Hampton L. Carson, this case stands as an "admirable illustration of the evolution of national authority."[47] It would also prove to be Lewis's longest case. In the end, Lewis would represent his clients, Gideon Olmsted and his associates, for thirty years.

Gideon Olmstead, Artimus White, Aquilla Rumsdale, and David Clark, citizens of the state of Connecticut, were captured by the British during the Revolutionary War and carried to Jamaica. While in Jamaica they were put on board the sloop *Active* to assist as mariners in navigating the vessel to New York—then in possession of the British—with a cargo of supplies for the fleets and armies of Great Britain. During the voyage, about September 6, 1778, Olmstead and his comrades rose up against the master and crew of the sloop, confining them to a cabin; the mutineers took command of the vessel and eventually headed for Egg Harbor, New Jersey. On September 8, now within sight of Egg Harbor, the *Active* was pursued and forcibly taken by Captain Thomas Houston, commander of the armed brig *Convention*, which belonged to the state of Pennsylvania. On September 15, the sloop was brought into the port of Philadelphia, where Houston claimed the *Active* as prize to the *Convention*. Captain James Josiah, master of the American privateer *Le Gerard*, too claimed a share of the capture, as his vessel had been in sight of, and by agreement cruising in concert with, the *Convention*. Olmstead and company also interposed a claim for the whole vessel and cargo as their exclusive prize.

The Pennsylvania State Court of Admiralty, however, adjudged Olmsted and associates only quarter of the net proceeds of the *Active* and its cargo, decreeing that the rest be divided between the state of Pennsylvania, the owners of the privateer, and the officers and crews of the *Convention* and the *Le Gerard*. Olmstead appealed his case to Congress. Benedict Arnold, who was looking for a means of obtaining large sums of cash, agreed to subsidize Olmstead's appeals in exchange for a portion of the spoils.[48] Arnold secured the services of James Wilson and William Lewis, who launched an appeal on behalf of Olmstead and his crewmen to the Court of Commissioners of Appeals in Prize Causes for the United States of America, where, on December 15, 1778, the sentence of the state court was reversed, and it was ordered and adjudged that the vessel and cargo should be considered the lawful prize of Olmstead and his friends, and that the marshal should pay the net proceeds of the said prize to them or their agent.[49]

The marshal, however, believed that the newly formed Admiralty Court of Pennsylvania had jurisdiction over the U.S. Court of Commissioners. He disregarded the ruling and paid the net proceeds to the state of Pennsylvania rather than to Olmstead's agent, leaving Olmstead and his friends the task of gaining access to their rightful money. This case was caught up in a quagmire of state politics for the next nine years and was still in the courts when the United States Constitution was passed in 1787. As Carson points out, the newly instituted constitution specified that "the judicial power of the United States was expressly extended to all cases of admiralty and maritime jurisdiction."[50] There was still no movement on the case. By 1808, the long-suffering Olmstead had applied to the U.S. Supreme Court for help in getting the state of Pennsylvania to move forward. The case was eventually heard in the U.S. Supreme Court, once again with William Lewis—joined by U.S. District Attorney Alexander Dallas—representing Olmstead and with the Attorney General of Pennsylvania, Walter Franklin, and Jared Ingersoll serving as opposing counsel. The court ruled in favor of Olmstead and his friends. However, the United States still needed to vindicate their authority over the state of Pennsylvania. Warrants were issued against those at the state level who had obstructed the federal process. Another long trial ensued, the outcome of which, according to Carson, was critical: "The priceless principle had been established that the Constitution and laws of the US shall be recognized as the supreme law of the land, 'and the judges in every state shall be bound thereby, anything in the Constitution or laws of any state to the contrary notwithstanding."[51] The legislature of a state could no longer annul the judgments, nor determine the jurisdiction, of the courts of the United States. Carson credits Lewis's "stubborn qualities as a legal pugilist" for the final outcome of the case.[52]

As the Revolutionary War progressed, Lewis continued to focus on his law practice, making a name for himself not just in Philadelphia but throughout the newly formed confederation. The country was only beginning to develop the laws that would meet the demands of a new and emerging federal government, and the necessity for skilled lawyers was increasing greatly. It was in this atmosphere that Lewis emerged not just as a leader but as an arbiter in developing the ethics of the bar as a whole.[53] As Binney puts it:

> The prominence of the City of Philadelphia as the seat of the Congress of the Confederation, and her superiority in population and commerce . . . may account, in some degree, for the diffusion of Mr. Lewis's celebrity, which partook of the distinction awarded to the City. But it was not in criminal law alone, that he was deemed, by other cities, to be the most able man at the Bar. He was a person of great intellectual ardor, and of a strong grasp of mind; and both in law and politics, and other matters too, he took firm hold of whatever interested him. His great devotion was, of course, to professional studies. He explored every field of law, common, constitutional, international, commercial, and maritime.[54]

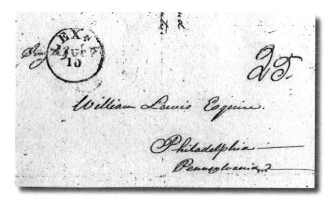

Photocopy of a letter sent to William Lewis. Original in Lewis family papers.

As legislation was created, Lewis worked diligently to ensure that the letter of the law was enforced, but he also remained true to his insistence on moderation and protection of the rights of the individual. Two cases highlight Lewis's mission during this time period. The first case, *Respublica v. Buffington* (1780), involved a Chester County yeoman, Joshua Buffington, who had been summoned by the Supreme Court of Pennsylvania for failure to respond to an earlier writ ordering him to appear before a local court.[55] Lewis, along with his co-counsel Jared Ingersoll, showed that the original writ contained serious errors that rendered it invalid. It had contained incorrect information, including an address that had never been associated with the defendant. Proving this error, Lewis showed that his client believed the writ had not been meant for him. The court agreed with the defense and dismissed the case. Lewis successfully showed that the Executive Council of the State of Pennsylvania was bound to "strictness . . . in the descriptions of all indictments."[56]

The case of Samuel Chapman is significant as an indicator of the toleration for dissenting viewpoints that was gradually developing at this time. The case represented a great stride toward fixing moderation as a state policy.[57] Born in Bucks County, Pennsylvania, just north of Philadelphia, Chapman joined the British military when his ship was captured at sea in December 1776. While later imprisoned in Massachusetts, Pennsylvania authorities had him extradited on a claim that he had not complied with a writ of attainder in June 1778. Chapman was charged with treason for fighting alongside the British. In his defense of Chapman, Lewis proved that there was no existing state government in December 1776; it was a time of civil unrest, and many colonists were still loyal to England. No allegiance, therefore, was due from Chapman. Chief Justice McKean agreed that, as no treason statutes existed at that time, there was no violation of any enforceable laws. Chapman was found not guilty.

As the initial wave of patriotic fervor dissipated, the citizens of Philadelphia turned to other sobering matters, while Lewis's work as a lawyer started to transition into new territory. The Revolution had taken its toll on an uncertain economy, leaving both winners and losers of those who had taken financial risks during that era. A large financial debt had been left in the wake of war. The Articles of Confederation, drafted by the Second Continental Congress and finally ratified in March of 1781, had done little to alleviate the pressure. The Articles provided for no division of legislative powers and actually left the majority of power with the states. A weak central (national) power, combined with Congress's inability to tax individuals, meant that the newly formed United States of America had no means to pay its debts. Additionally, Congress couldn't regulate commerce, leaving the states to compete against one another.

Americans would start to weigh and debate the need to adopt "mechanical inventions, national currency, banks, corporations, steamboats, the extension of market relations into rural areas, and so many other changes in the youthful republic's bountiful promise."[58] The economy of the new nation needed to grow—but how, and in what form? How might the economy be regulated? The major driving force of the transition from the traditional precommercial economy toward an increasingly market-oriented society was the burgeoning alliance formed between merchants and the legal profession.[59] It was in Philadelphia that much of this transformation originated. As the second-largest English-speaking city (just behind London), it served not just as the seat of government but as the most important American market. In the alliance between business and law, the Philadelphia lawyer would become integral. William Lewis was a leading attorney in the city and would by the end of the eighteenth century "become nationally known for his unsurpassed knowledge of commercial law and the booming brilliance of his oratory."[60]

Well-known Philadelphia merchant Robert Waln, hearing Lewis discuss the commercial relations between America and Europe at a dinner party where they were both guests, observed, "Mr. Lewis seems as familiar with commercial affairs as if he had been the head of a counting-house all his life." "Let me tell you, sir," replied Lewis, "that a competent lawyer knows *everything* that a merchant does, *and a great deal more.*"[61]

Lewis was becoming a revered tactician in many realms—property law, treason, commercial law, and more. He was highly regarded for his dedication to the justice that law was meant to serve. The postrevolutionary years were a time of development in the courts, and Lewis continued to keep the legal system on its toes. His law office remained busy, with more mundane transactions often handled by one of the office clerks.

What stands out in the cases that Lewis took on during and just after the Revolution is that he was resolute in his focus; he did not do just what he had to in order to ensure that his clients received a fair trial, but he also ensured that the courts were operating in the highest order. In *Rivers v. Walker*, Lewis, arguing for the defendant, charged that the notice of time and place of the referees' meeting had not been delivered to his client but, rather, to the client's attorney. The court ruled that the notice must be sent to the party and consequently dismissed the case.[62]

In *Hagner v. Musgrove*, Lewis challenged the proceedings when his clients (the parties to the suit) were asked to leave the witness examination due to flaring tempers.[63] The court agreed with Lewis and ruled that all parties have the right to attend witness examinations. This case helped establish civil law to correct the perceived injustices in common law.

The case of Robert Steele represents another important step in establishing the role and practice of the courts. Steele was accused of robbery, apprehended, and brought before the court in Philadelphia in 1785. In his defense of Steele, Lewis sought to show that the court had failed to accurately describe Steele's person or to establish his residency in a particular town.[64] Lewis was unable to win an acquittal, but his argument highlighted the court's imperative to ensure accuracy on the part of the Attorney General (who served the writ of capias). Members of the Executive Council had concerns over these details and those of similar cases, and after a lengthy discussion, Steele was granted a pardon.

While Lewis made sure the courts followed the letter of the law in their conviction and execution of an outlaw robber, he had no sympathy for someone who would use the courts to commit fraud—even if that individual was an influential citizen and his own client. Brown relates an incident in which Lewis became aware during the trial that his client had not disclosed all the facts and had indeed committed fraud.[65] At this point, he narrates, Lewis threw his brief into the air and declined to address the bench. "Will you NOT speak?" the client asked. "No sir," was Lewis's response. His client demanded, "What then have I paid you for?" Lewis replied, "You have paid me that you might have justice done, and justice will now be done without my further interference."[66]

During this period, Lewis also served as the attorney for the Finance and Marine Departments of the American Confederation. In January 1783, he drafted legislation on behalf of Robert Morris, who served as the Superintendent of Finance, in efforts to recover debts and property owed to the United States.[67] In the years following, Lewis became an authority in cases of debt recovery and the complicated issues surrounding the various stakeholders.

Three

Abolition Work:

A Tireless Advocate Fights to Gain Freedom for All

William Lewis's devotion to justice along with his dedication to the rights of the individual attracted him to one of the greatest efforts of his time—the abolition of slavery. Lewis's opportunity to make the greatest impact in this area came in 1779, when the Pennsylvania state legislature, in the words of William Primrose, "took the lead in a public declaration of the illegality of that odious and disgraceful subjugation of fellow creatures which had so long stained the character of America. A provision, perhaps necessarily imperfect, but carried as far as then appeared practicable, was made in favor of the descendents of Africa, by which a chance of emancipation to those then living, and a certainty of it to their issue, was secured."[68]

What Primrose refers to as a "public declaration" was the Act for the Gradual Abolition of Slavery in Pennsylvania, which was approved in March 1780. Over time, several men have been credited as authors of the act, including William Lewis, Thomas Paine, and George Bryan. Paine, who had created a stir with his incendiary and most popular pamphlet, *Common Sense*, was certainly known as a wordsmith. George Bryan was also well known as a successful businessman and legislator and as acting president of the board of the Supreme Executive Council of Pennsylvania. He addressed the Pennsylvania General Assembly in August 1778, calling for the prohibition of the importation of slaves into Pennsylvania.[69] Some, such as historian Gary Nash, contend that Bryan "shepherded the bill through the legislature," as his position would have allowed him the opportunity to do so. But Nash also believes that the actual drafting of the act was most likely a committee effort to which Lewis provided invaluable legal advice.[70]

Horace Binney—who as a young lawyer witnessed Lewis in action and would go on to his own esteemed law career, including serving as a U.S. Congressman—dealt with the question of authorship more directly:

> [Lewis] was much interested in the abolition of slavery within the State of Pennsylva. Since his death, some questions have been raised in regard to the part, whether active or consultative, that he took in promoting the Act of 1st March, 1780, "for the gradual abolition of slavery in Pennsylvania;" and I do not mean to raise any question of my own. But I am perfectly clear that, in his lifetime, and at the beginning of this century, when others who may now be thought to have been actors in the matter, were living, Mr. Lewis was currently spoken of, at the Bar, as the draughtsman of that Act.[71]

A number of later publications also credited Lewis as the draftsman of the act, including Scharf and Westcott's *History of Philadelphia* (1884). According to their entry on William Lewis:

> Mr. Lewis confined himself more strictly to the law and paid less attention to politics than most of his contemporaries of equal professional rank, but he merits notice and remembrance in politics as the draftsman of the famous act of 1780, abolishing slavery,—the first act of the kind passed in any county.[72]

Bryan might have turned to Lewis, the young, hard-working lawyer who had already gained a reputation as an avid abolitionist, to take on the arduous work of drafting the bill. Regardless of who did what, drafting the act was only the beginning. Once it became law, it played a critical role in eliminating slavery over time in Pennsylvania. Lewis would certainly have relied heavily on its provisions for litigation.[73] Further, his unprecedented knowledge of the act's wording and intent would make him the authority on enforcing it through the courts.

The 1780 act's preamble replicated the pervasive revolutionary rhetoric of the time by arguing that slavery was similar to the relationship that had existed between the colonists and England. Like many abolitionists in the 1770s had argued, the 1780 act claimed that having achieved independence from Britain, the "free" citizens of the new nation had a duty to extend that freedom further. This attitude might have only been possible at that particular time in Philadelphia—a diversely populated, large port city with an active citizenry of Quakers, who had expelled slavery from their society. It was also a place with relatively few slaves in comparison with other states, allowing the goal of freedom to be relatively attainable in ways it wasn't elsewhere.

When passed, the act abolished perpetual servitude and provided freedom at age twenty-eight for those children born to slave mothers after November 1, 1780. The law also required slave owners to register their slaves by that same date and forbade new slaves from being brought into Pennsylvania as residents. However, it did recognize that slavery existed in almost all of the other thirteen states and therefore allowed nonresident masters to bring slaves into Pennsylvania for temporary residency of no more than six months, thereby abolishing perpetual bondage but continuing its presence in the state; in actuality, slavery in Pennsylvania would not truly end until the 1840s.

Act of the Legislature of Pennsylvania,

For the gradual Abolition of Slavery;

Passed March 1st, 1780.

SECTION 1. WHEN we contemplate our abhorrence of that condition, to which the arms and tyranny of Great Britain were exerted to reduce us—when we look back on the variety of dangers to which we have been exposed, and how miraculously our wants in many instances have been supplied, and our deliverances wrought, when even hope and human fortitude have become unequal to the conflict—we are unavoidably led to a serious and grateful sense of the manifold blessings which we have undeservedly received from the hand of that Being, from whom every good and perfect gift cometh. Impressed with these ideas, we conceive that it is our duty, and we rejoice that it is in our power, to extend a portion of that freedom to others, which hath been extended to us; and a release from that state of thraldom, to which we ourselves were tyrannically doomed, and from which we have now every prospect of being delivered. It is not for us to enquire why, in the creation of mankind, the inhabitants of the several parts of the earth were distinguished by a difference in feature or complexion It is sufficient to know that all are the work of an Almighty Hand. We find, in the distribution of the human species, that the most fertile as well as the most barren parts of the earth are inhabited by men of complexions different from ours, and from each other; from whence we may reasonably, as well as religiously, infer, that he who placed them in their various situations, hath extended equally his care and protection to all, and that it becometh not us to counteract his mercies. We esteem it a peculiar blessing granted to us, that we are enabled this day to add one more step to universal civilization, by removing, as much as possible, the sorrows of those who have lived in undeserved bondage, and from which, by the assumed authority of the kings of Great-Britain, no effectual, legal relief could be obtained. Weaned by a long course of experience from those narrow prejudices and partialities we had imbibed, we find our hearts enlarged with kindness and benevolence towards men of all conditions and nations; and we conceive ourselves at this particular period extraordinarily called upon, by the blessings which we have received, to manifest the sincerity of our profession, and to give a substantial proof of our gratitude.

Preamble to the Act of Gradual Abolition in Pennsylvania. Pennsylvania Abolition Society Papers, Historical Society of Pennsylvania.

In order to ensure that slave owners upheld the letter and intent of the new law, the Pennsylvania Society of Promoting the Abolition of Slavery and the Relief of Free Negroes Unlawfully Held in Bondage and for Improving the Condition of the African Race was formed in 1784. Otherwise known as the Pennsylvania Abolition Society, or PAS, this society was based on an earlier incarnation called the Society for the Protection of Free Blacks, which had been founded by a small group of Quakers in April of 1775 to help expand opposition to slavery. This first group disbanded at the beginning of the Revolutionary War. While the original intent of the PAS was to assist illegally enslaved blacks, they began to place a new emphasis on abolishing slavery by interrupting the slave trade and passing gradual abolition legislation in other parts of the country. William Lewis was not a founding member of the organization, but he joined the cause early on and immediately took on the majority of their legal burdens.[74] His efforts were honored in May 1786, when Lewis was presented with a three-pint silver can inscribed with a motto descriptive of the intentions of the Society. It was said that he accepted the token as a sign of respect rather than as a gratuity for services rendered, as "he declared his determination never to receive a pecuniary reward" for this work.[75]

By 1787, as members of the Constitutional Convention met in Philadelphia to debate the new federal constitution, the PAS had further organized and increased its membership to include individuals from seven additional states (forty-two members), Great Britain (twelve members) and France (five members including the Marquis de Lafayette).[76] By this time, the group consisted of more than just a handful of Quaker shopkeepers, artisans, and tailors; the Pennsylvania members totaled 227 and had gained the support of patriot leaders such as Benjamin Rush, William Rawle, and Caspar Wistar. Most importantly, the PAS had gained the attention of Benjamin Franklin, who, having just returned to America after twelve years abroad, was happy to lend his name to the organization by becoming its president. The additional officers named at that time were James Pemberton and Jonathan Penrose (as co-vice presidents), Benjamin Rush and Caspar Wistar (as secretaries), James Starr (as treasurer), and William Lewis, Myers Fisher, William Rawle, and John D. Coxe (as counselors). The universal recognition of Franklin's name, along with the prominence of its officers, would help the PAS achieve even further prestige. As the first abolition society in the western world, the group's constitution informed the world that their members would "use such means as are in their power to extend the blessings of freedom to every part of the human race."[77] By reaching out and sharing information with their English and French counterparts, the PAS would achieve international influence in their efforts to end the slave trade. Back at home, their goals moved beyond abolition and freedom for those enslaved unlawfully to include improvement of conditions in the African American community at large. This, they believed, could best be achieved by building schools where black children could be educated.[78]

By 1789, Franklin's influence helped the PAS gain official incorporation in Pennsylvania, thereby achieving greater legal standing in the state. Word of William Lewis and his work for the PAS spread quickly, drawing many blacks to the area in hopes of winning their freedom. Lewis's neighbor Thomas Harrison, a Quaker tailor on Third Street, was known to provide temporary refuge to those seeking freedom. This close proximity to Lewis's office at "Fort Wilson" certainly made communication between Lewis and his potential clients quite feasible.

During this time, the Pennsylvania abolitionists ran the most effective legal aid system for endangered African Americans anywhere. Their strategy for success rested on the twin pillars of petitioning and legal work.[79] As stated in section 5 of the PAS constitution, "the business of the counsellors shall be to explain the laws and constitutions of the states, which relate to the emancipation of slaves, and to urge their claims to freedom, when legal, before such persons or courts, as are authorized to decide upon them."

Lewis and his fellow counselors worked tirelessly, utilizing any and all tactics they could lawfully devise to gain freedom for their clients. In a March 1787 letter to David Barclay, Tench Coxe reported on the activities of the PAS:

> we have sometimes been under the necessity of pursuing our duty thro the medium of law, in which a very able counselor, William Lewis, Esq., who from principle, early espoused the cause of these people, frequently renders us his disinterested services. There are others among the gentlemen of that profession who have stept forward in their behalf sometimes unsolicited, and often without reward. Many cases have ended to perfect satisfaction, upwards of one hundred persons having been restored to their liberty since the revival of the institution.[80]

Despite its increased and high profile membership, the PAS was working within a society where most of the population was indifferent to and at times quite hostile toward the rights of African Americans or people of color in general. The PAS's activities brought it into conflict with hundreds of Americans, including George Washington. He wrote to his friend Robert Morris in Philadelphia to complain about "a vexatious law-suit" brought by "a Society of Quakers" who attempted to liberate a slave belonging to Philip Dalby of Alexandria, Virginia.[81] Washington speculated that citizens who owned slaves would simply refuse to visit Philadelphia should this type of lawsuit continue.

Dalby had come to Philadelphia with his servant, Francis Belt, only to have the PAS institute legal proceedings to obtain Belt's freedom. Belt, born in Maryland, was the illegitimate child of an unmarried slave woman and a white man. Lewis took on the case, arguing two key points: first, that Pennsylvania law did not support slavery and did not recognize Maryland's laws to the extent that a third party was injured. Second, Lewis argued that in common law, a child's status followed that of his father, in which case Belt should be free. Of course, the court's acceptance of this logic would have freed all children fathered by white men. The court declined Lewis's logic and ultimately ruled in favor of Dalby, but only after he was forced to expend a considerable amount of time and money to prove his claim of ownership of Belt. Dalby's victory was short lived, however, as within the year it was reported that Belt had escaped his master in Virginia and was presumed en route to Philadelphia.[82]

Of the many cases argued by Lewis and his fellow counselors on behalf of slaves, they were most successful in those suits that involved noncompliance with the Act of Gradual Abolition. Many masters were negligent or simply ignored the requirements of the act. Samuel Moore, for example, held three slaves, whom he did not properly register as required by law. Lewis successfully claimed their immediate freedom under the law as the penalty for failure to properly register them. Likewise, Lewis argued for the freedom of Betsy, Cato, and Isaac, the children of Moore's freed slaves, who were still with their master and also had not been properly registered. Despite a split decision among the judges of the Supreme Court of Pennsylvania, their free status was confirmed.[83] Finally, in *Republica v. The Gaoler of Philadelphia County* Lewis successfully used the act to win the freedom of Robert, who had been brought into Pennsylvania in 1779 as a slave for life.[84] Robert had never been registered by his master. Ultimately, he became a ward of the guardians of the poor, who indentured him as a servant until twenty-eight years of age. Those guardians attempted to prove they did not have to abide by the rules of the original master. Lewis proved otherwise.

Along with efforts to have it repealed, the Act for Gradual Abolition had become the target of "all the mischiefs and subtle evasions which artful and unprincipled men are too apt to embrace." In 1788 a petition was introduced into the Pennsylvania General Assembly to address the evasive practices of unscrupulous slave owners:

> *Resolved*, That a Committee be appointed to bring in a bill to explain and amend the Act, entitled, "An Act for the gradual abolition of slavery."

> *Ordered*, That Messrs. Lewis, Wynkoop, Kennedy, Piper and Lollar, be a Committee to bring in a bill conformably to the foregoing resolution.[85]

Lewis, then a member of the Pennsylvania House, was appointed to a committee formed to further explain the act's intentions and to close its loopholes. Jacob Hiltzheimer took notes of the House proceedings on March 28. As he recalled, "in the house the bill for the gradual abolition of slavery was in its third reading. After dinner I . . . drank a glass of wine with General Mifflin . . . who attended the [Pennsylvania General] Assembly with other Friends to urge passage of the bill. The House met again in the afternoon and the bill was passed."[86] Thus, the Pennsylvania General Assembly passed An Act to Explain and Amend an Act, entitled, "An Act for the Gradual Abolition of Slavery."

Lewis's work on behalf of the PAS—whether through representation or submissions of legal opinion—would continue throughout the rest of his career. Lewis worked tirelessly to ensure that slave owners operated under the letter of the law. In 1793, Lewis was asked to weigh in on the question of whether the children of Kitty, an escaped slave of Betty Chitton, were slave or free. They had all been born in Pennsylvania after the passage of the 1780 act. Lewis's written opinion was concise and straightforward in the extreme, almost as if he could not believe that the matter at hand was still being debated: "I believe that about twenty years ago I gave a similar opinion to the foregoing ones [those of his colleagues] and am fully satisfied that it was perfectly correct." The opinions given were all in agreement—whether or not their mother was an escaped slave did not matter; under the statutes of the act, the children were free.[87]

Especially vexing to Lewis were those cases where slaves were shipped in and out of Pennsylvania to avoid the six-month residency period that would trigger a slave's freedom. To Lewis, the subterfuge of an owner temporarily leaving the state or sending his slaves out of town just prior to the deadline was just cause for action—even in those cases where he knew the owners personally.

One of these instances came in mid-1790 with the arrival in Philadelphia of a sudden influx of French refugees escaping the violent slave rebellion in Santo Domingo. A Mrs. Chambre had arrived in town along with two of her female slaves, Magdalen and Zare. As she did not properly register these women as per requirements, William Lewis petitioned for their freedom on behalf of the PAS.[88] After five months and three weeks, Mrs. Chambre departed for New Jersey, taking her slaves with her. Lewis found it impossible to prove that Mrs. Chambre had moved the women simply to evade the six-month limit, so he decided instead to focus his case on how the time was measured, asking the court to use a lunar month calculation instead of the calendar month. Lewis hoped his interpretation of the act would enable the court enough leeway to show compassion for these women.[89] The court declined, unanimously stating that the legislature had intended that calendar months were to be used in calculating time of residence. Obviously, in his desperation to free these women, Lewis was, in effect, "making things up." But what's more intriguing is that Lewis was willing to put his reputation on the line in such a manner; while the rest of America worried that by allowing these particular slaves—and their reputed violent ways—into the country, they were tempting fate that their necks might be the next ones slashed.

One of the most curious freedom cases William Lewis dealt with involved the prominent Chew family—a family Lewis had long associated with on both a social and business level. Harriet Chew Carroll had returned to her family's residence in Philadelphia from her marriage home in Maryland, accompanied by her servant Charity Castle. Well aware that Charity would gain freedom after a six-month residency, Harriet's brother Benjamin Chew, Jr., wrote to her father-in-law, Charles Carroll, to ask for help in making arrangements for Charity to vacate Philadelphia.[90] According to his letter, Charity had become greatly agitated upon hearing of her impending return to Homewood, Harriet's home in Baltimore, stating that she would go anywhere but there—even claiming that she would rather be sold or sent to a remote destination. Charity went on to tell Harriet something so shocking that Benjamin declared in his letter that it would distress him to repeat it and would not offer any details except *"suffice it to say that from the woman's account it would be improper to place her at Homewood where attempts have been essayed that Delicacy forbids me to particularize."*[91] It should be noted that present-day research indicates that Harriet had returned to Philadelphia with her children because her husband was allegedly a drunk and an abuser—thus, Harriet would have been hard-pressed not to accept the word of Charity over that of her own husband.

Benjamin's proposed solution to Mr. Carroll was to exchange one of Carroll's own servants for that of his son's property. Benjamin also reminded Carroll that they had only a few more weeks to get Charity out of Pennsylvania before she would be considered free under Pennsylvania law. It appears that the night before a courier arrived in Philadelphia to collect Charity and transport her out of state, she suffered a fall while bringing in firewood from the yard. It was said she was found some time later, bloody and unconscious, by another servant. Charity was attended by a physician and confined to bed. The physician informed the courier that Charity would not be in any condition to leave the Chew household for two months, as doing so would endanger her life. About a month later (in November), Dr. Nathaniel Chapman made a written recommendation to Benjamin Chew informing him that despite Charity's improvement, her situation was still fragile enough that she should remain in the Chew household throughout the winter.

Knowing that Charity would gain her freedom while wintering in Philadelphia, the Chew family solicited legal opinions in hopes that their circumstance would be viewed as an exception under the law. William Lewis submitted an opinion that he intended for presentation directly to Harriet Carroll. Dated November 29, 1814, and signed by Lewis, it read:

> It is stated to me that Charity the Slave of Mr Chas Carroll of the State of Maryland was brought to the City of Philadelphia in May last by her Mistress Mrs Carroll who came on a Visit to her Friends & Relations and that when Charity had been detained here by her Mistress nearly six months she met with an accident which occasioned an indisposition that prevented her return to Maryland until after six months and more

had expired and that she hath been detained here ever since.

    If the above Statement is correct I am clearly of opinion that Charity is free and that she cannot be legally sent to Maryland—I however wish this Opinion to be shewn to Mrs Caroll in order that if she shall not be satisfied she may have an opportunity of taking the opinion of her own Counsel.[92]

Benjamin Chew replied to Lewis, confirming that his sister had read the opinion; he then launched into a detailed recapitulation of the proceedings. Lewis replied—in true form—the next day:

> your letter of yesterday occasions no alteration of my opinion. Indeed all the material facts mentioned in it, were known to me before.
>
>   I have no doubt of her having been well treated, if the Case may appear to be a hard one on the part of Mr Carroll, I cannot but consider hers [Charity's] abundantly more so, from her *State of Slavery &* as is probably the case, accident made her a Slave, accident had made her free, and it seems right that she should avail herself of it.

This response is quintessential Lewis. His bottom line was that Charity remained in Pennsylvania for longer than six months; therefore, according to the law, she was free. Benjamin Chew requested a second opinion and forwarded a description of the proceedings, along with Lewis's opinion, to William Rawle.[93] Rawle focused on the wording of the law in the clause "retained in this State longer than six months." By his opinion, Charity was not "retained" by her master; rather, the master had been obliged to submit to Charity's need to stay in bed. She had not, therefore, acquired freedom under the law.

    Ironically, Harriett Carroll's husband, Charles Carroll, Jr., informed his father that he did not wish to litigate his claim of ownership in the "prejudiced Jury of Pennsylvania." Even if he won, he would gain nothing but a slave whose "malice and falsehood" would preclude her from remaining in his household. He ended his letter by claiming, "I care not what becomes of the unhappy Wretch—I will give Myself no further pain about Her, Yet reserving to Myself the right of ever—claiming Her as My Slave, for the presumption of which, I have the *learned* opinions of Mr. Chew & Mr. Rawle."[94]

    Charles Jr.'s final determination was to sell Charity to her own husband—or to anyone who might wish to prosecute the suit—for three-hundred dollars. Lewis's last known letter concerning the case was sent to Harriet Carroll on December 24, 1814:

> Madam,
>
>   In consequence of your letter to me of today, I have advised the Husband of Charity to take her to himself, and that Mr. Carroll may have an opportunity of claiming her in such legal manner as he may think proper, I have directed, that she shall at all times be forthcoming when properly called for.
>
>   I am, Madam, with great respect
>   Your humble Servt
>   W Lewis

We have no definitive knowledge of what happened to Charity Castle. The story is loaded with intrigue and unanswered questions: her accident, the servant who found her, the physician who treated her, her "unmentionable" tale from her time at Homewood . . . and whether, in the end, she was able to walk away a free woman. Because of the actions of William Lewis, it seems she just might have.

Included in Lewis's estate papers is his personal copy of the "Constitution and Act of Incorporation of the Pennsylvania Society for Promoting the Abolition of Slavery, and the Relief of Free Negroes, Unlawfully Held in Bondage, and for Improving the Condition of the African Race." This copy—printed in 1800 by Philadelphian J. Ormrod and held together by a piece of red ribbon—contains Lewis's signature at the top and the notation "Black Acts" on a separate page, perhaps noting the inclusion of "The Acts of the General Assembly of Pennsylvania for the Gradual Abolition of Slavery, and the Acts of the Congress of the United States, Respecting Slaves and Slave-Trade."[95] Despite the fact he had by this date no doubt memorized the contents, this much-worn copy was certainly consulted as Lewis conferred his opinion on the Charity Castle case and others, thus insuring that every letter of the law was addressed. Charity and those who came before her certainly had no better friend than William Lewis, as his former student and close friend Major William Jackson noted: "The cases in which he [Lewis] was concerned to protect the Africans from bondage are too many to enumerate–they would fill a volume." William Primrose called Lewis "a champion of this cause," for:

> With a voluntary dereliction of all professional emolument, he strenuously and boldly pursued oppression into its artful recesses and succeeded in securing to the injured African all the protection to be found in the text of the law. Thousands of the present generation [1820] of colored people are unconsciously indebted to him for his exertion, anxiety, and exposure, before they were born.[96]

Four

Enlightened Statesman:

An Avid Federalist Advances the Cause

By 1787 Lewis became politically active in his own right when he was elected to the General Assembly of Pennsylvania. Of particular interest to the assembly at that time was the question of whether or not the new federal constitution should be adopted. In September, the Federal Constitutional Convention met in Philadelphia. It had been eleven years since the signing of the Declaration of Independence. And while it was generally agreed that the Articles of the Confederation were ineffectual, there was still widespread distrust among the representatives of the thirteen states. Chief Justice McKean confessed in a letter to John Adams written in April 1787 that "popular opinion is, that we should be very jealous of conferring power on any man or body of men . . . indeed we seem afraid to enable any one to do good lest he should do evil."[97] At this point there was no central currency and no common laws among the states, but the thought of consolidating power—creating a centralized government—was daunting to most. Still, the document that came out of the convention achieved several economic objectives: first, it provided the political environment necessary for a single, free-trade area within the nation; second, it made the federal government a potentially effective instrument of foreign policy; and third, it recognized the primacy of property rights and the freedom of individuals to acquire and transfer property. Further, the Constitution gave the federal government the exclusive right to regulate both foreign and interstate trade and the exclusive right to levy import duties. Elected president of the convention, General George Washington had sat in a prominent chair throughout the difficult proceedings; the delegates had taken notice of the sun painted on the part of the chair that emerged just above the general's head. On difficult days some had commented that the sun appeared to be setting, but on the last day of the convention, Benjamin Franklin settled the question when he said, "I have the happiness to know that it is indeed a rising, not a setting sun."

The Constitution would now need to be ratified by each of the thirteen states. The work of the convention delegates was now to return to their home states to sell the Constitution and what it represented to their own constituents. The question remained: could the delegates convince their constituents to ratify a federal constitution? Would the government of the United States be a republic?

By November 6, Pennsylvania became the first state to call a convention to measure the pros and cons of the newly proposed federal constitution. As a member of the Pennsylvania General Assembly, William Lewis took his place among those debating its merits. He was also appointed to the Ratification Committee, so he was serving double duty. The process required for all of thirteen states to ratify the Constitution, with a quorum of votes at the national level, would take two years. Emerging political affiliations would become ever more important as those representing each state started to weigh the effects of this new federal constitution and how it would affect their abilities to govern at the state level. Emerging political associations would increase in importance.

In Pennsylvania, the arguments between the Conservatives and the Radicals (also called Constitutionalists, a name held over from the Pennsylvania state constitutional convention of 1776) of western Pennsylvania became even more pointed. Those in favor of adopting the federal constitution would soon become known as the Federalist Party. Back in New York where he had served as a Constitutional delegate, Alexander Hamilton (along with James Madison and John Jay) started to write a series of articles that would become known as the Federalist Papers; these essays advocated for the ratification of the Constitution. The general Federalist view, as it became known, was an expansive view of the Constitution, for a nation as a unified entity, but contrasted by the guarantee of the greatest personal liberty for each individual. This was exactly what Lewis and his fellow Philadelphia lawyers had hoped to achieve: a set of principles regarding individuals' rights accompanied by written laws restraining government. This was the combination of individual rights and government oversight that would allow the new nation to become the market-oriented society these men had envisioned. The contrasting view came from Thomas Jefferson and his followers, who would later become known as the Democratic-Republicans. They favored states' rights over a centralized power, and they believed in the primacy of the farmer over merchants, bankers, and industrialists.

While William Lewis and his fellow state Constitutional convention delegates took up their debates in the State House, Philadelphians debated in drawing rooms and taverns across the city. Some even took to the streets to make their intentions known to the opposition. It was reported that three members of the Pennsylvania Supreme Executive Council and four members of the house—all noted Anti-Federalists—were awakened at their place of lodging in the middle of the night by a noisy mob throwing rocks and yelling disparaging remarks. Cries of "Here the damn rascals live who do all the mischief," and "They ought to be all hanged" rose up from the street.[98] City dwellers tended to be in favor of ratifying the federal constitution and did not take kindly to those opposed. The incident set off its own heated debate when the matter was brought to the attention of the House along with a resolution recommending that the Supreme Executive Council offer a reward for information on the perpetrators. At question was who had the jurisdiction to do what. Was this a local issue that should be left up to the city troop (the police)? To Lewis, the questions at hand were matters of constitutionality. Was this a matter for the Supreme Executive Council or for the courts to handle? And what were the rights of the individuals who wished to express their opinions? Was this merely a power struggle between these emerging factions? Lewis was concerned that the rights of the individual should not be suppressed by the government, but he was also concerned lest the rights of the executive and judicial branches be usurped by the legislative branch. Even McKean, who had earlier sided with the Constitutionalists, confessed to Adams that the proper constitutional balance had not been met with Pennsylvania's current government. "The legislature is too powerful for the executive and judicial branches of government . . . it can too easily make laws, and too easily alter or repeal them."[99]

Legislative authority was addressed again a few days later, when the group debated setting a quorum number of delegates for ratification during the convention. An amendment was proposed that would require two-thirds attendance for a quorum. Those opposed were worried that delegates from the near counties might get together and make decisions before those from further counties might arrive. Lewis's reported response was that he had confidence in the delegates chosen and that they no doubt "wish their meeting to be as full as possible, in order to give dignity and force to their decisions, which a partial representation must of consequence diminish."[100] As it turns out, the issue of the quorum number would become quite significant when it came time for the delegates to cast their votes.

In the meantime, the convention would be warned that it had not been called to legislate, to inquire into the powers of the late convention, or to alter or amend its work; "the present task [was] simply to ratify and confirm, or, upon due consideration, reject in the whole, the system of federal government."[101] The Federalists sought to gain quick acceptance of the plan while the momentum was theirs, hoping to influence other states. They saw no need for extended debate or delays. Anti-Federalists viewed the process in the exact opposite light. When it was time to call a vote, the convention found that indeed, they did not have a quorum of delegates on hand—they were two delegates short. In an attempt to slow down the process, several of the Anti-Federalists decided to hide out in their lodgings to prevent the vote. Upon figuring out the plan, members of the opposition took matters into their own hands, storming the boarding house where they knew several delegates were presently staying and "kidnapping" two of them. Once these delegates were delivered back to the State House, the quorum was achieved, and the vote was taken. On December 12, 1787, the convention formally ratified the federal constitution, becoming the second state to do so. The vote split along Federalist and Anti-Federalist lines, with forty-six votes in favor and twenty-three in opposition.[102] Much to the disappointment of the Pennsylvania legislature, Delaware was actually the first state to officially ratify the constitution on December 7 with a unanimous vote. The Constitution only required ratification by nine of the thirteen states. New Hampshire became the ninth state to ratify on June 21, 1788.

The new government had now been ratified. On the fourth of July the citizens of Philadelphia celebrated the Federalist victory in their usual style. Dr. Benjamin Rush recalled the scene a few days later in a letter to Elias Boudinot: "The constitution was carried by a great law officer [Chief Justice McKean] to denote the elevation of the government of law and justice above everything else." In fact, McKean rode on a carriage over twenty feet long, its rear wheels eight feet in diameter, with a replica of the federal eagle over thirteen feet high and thirteen feet long.[103] The Anti-Federalists were not impressed. One particularly unfriendly observation of the parade noted: "the car was as high as the houses. . . . Some wondered how the judges got into the car, if by a ladder or upon the people's shoulders."[104]

Comments such as these created disagreements regarding the proper role of the press in a free republican society and the extent of legal change necessitated by the Revolution. Early in 1788, Eleazer Oswald had published a number of articles critical of Andrew Brown, another prominent Philadelphia Federalist. Asserting that the articles libeled him, Brown hired William Lewis to sue Oswald if he did not provide the names of the authors of the offending articles. While admitting that the articles suffered from the invective nature of the current high political ferment, Oswald refused to divulge the names and even went on to state that he believed Brown's actions were politically motivated and backed by Federalists hoping to destroy his *Independent Gazetteer*—an anti-Federalist publication. Brown went ahead with the prosecution. After preliminary arguments, Oswald was allowed to return to his paper as editor, and despite the impending trial, he immediately published a discussion of the issues in his *Gazetteer*. He did not go easy on the Court or Chief Justice McKean. Incensed by his actions and probably still upset by Oswald's earlier published personal attacks, some dating back to 1782, McKean charged the editor with contempt of the court and with libeling the court and its justices. Oswald was fined ten pounds and sentenced to one month in jail with an admonishment from McKean: "your circumstances are small, but your offense is great."[105]

Oswald complained that McKean had perverted the doctrine of libel, a doctrine "incompatible with law and liberty, and at once destructive of the privileges of a free country."[106] The situation encouraged a rash of articles in the Philadelphia newspapers. Bitter over his treatment and convinced that he had gained the public's support, Oswald sought the impeachment of three justices: McKean, Rush, and Atlee. His hatred of McKean was so great by this time that it was said that only a public hanging of the chief justice would satisfy him.[107]

Oswald's memorial calling for legislative redress came before the Assembly on September 5, 1788. William Lewis, unsympathetic to Oswald, moved that the House sit as an inquest rather than forming a committee to investigate the charges. "If the Judges of the [Pennsylvania] Supreme Court are guilty of violating and disregarding the Constitution and the laws of the State," he argued, "they ought to be immediately presented before the proper tribunal and punished."[108] He also warned that the investigation was to determine innocence as well as culpability. McKean, for his part, welcomed a public investigation and thought "Lewis [was] so well acquainted with every particular that there [would] be no occasion for anything other than that he should be heard."[109] In the end, despite legal advice from William Findlay and widespread and growing criticism of McKean, Oswald's move to impeach the three judges did not garner enough support in the Assembly to move forward.

While growing issues such as freedom of the press were taken up in the discussion of the Bill of Rights at the federal level, William Lewis turned his attentions to the pressing matters of state politics. Reelected to represent Philadelphia in the Pennsylvania General Assembly, Lewis joined with his fellow Conservatives to once again call for a new state constitution. This time the group was successful, as the General Assembly called together a State Constitutional Convention for November 17, 1789, to review the issue. The Conservatives hoped that the review would provide them the opportunity to create an entirely new constitution that could replace the provisional document enacted just after the Declaration of Independence. This convention numbered among its members the most distinguished men of the times, including some of the best political and legal talent from both factions. On the Conservative side, William Lewis was joined by James Wilson, Thomas McKean, and Samuel Sitgreaves. The Constitutionalists were represented by William Findley, John Smilie, and Albert Gallatin.[110] Thought to be the most fair and tolerant, Thomas Mifflin was voted president of the convention. The Constitutionalists' approach to this convention was much more amenable than it had been in the past. They did not want to be accused of being Anti-Federalist, as they had been previously labeled for not voting for the federal constitution. That fact, coupled with the reality that the Conservatives had a slight majority, meant that the convention started out a bit smoother than might have initially been expected.[111]

Lewis was one of five chosen to draft the rules and regulations for the conduct of the business at the convention. Some concern arose about what would be recorded, as the records would be published. Those in attendance hoped to avoid reigniting the animosity between the Radicals (Constitutionalists) from the west and the Conservatives in the city. They worried that the published records could provide just such a spark, particularly if they indicated disagreements following rigid party lines. Lewis made efforts to keep specific names out of the official reports, hoping to blur the positions between the emerging party lines. By December 9, the rules were finalized and adopted. McKean was voted Chairman of the Committee of the Whole and Lewis was once again included in a committee (this time of nine) to draft amendments to restructure the Pennsylvania government. McKean reported on recommended changes, which included a bicameral legislature, a single executive, and judicial appointments.

Lewis consistently voted in a Conservative manner—seeking more centralized control of government by advocating for a return to a single executive with an elite upper house and a larger lower house, thereby reducing the influence of the masses. This formulation would be more in line with the federal constitution. The Conservatives also hoped to increase Senate terms from four to six years and to make the Senate an elite body by requiring qualification for office—ownership of five hundred dollars of real estate or personal property—but they were overwhelmingly defeated. Lewis and McKean in particular were quite vocal in their efforts to afford the Pennsylvania Supreme Court justices some control over their cases. By late January, 1790, the new constitution was accepted by the convention, and January 23, a committee was formed (once again including Lewis) to draft a schedule for implementation. By February 26, 1790, the convention convened with a draft of the new Pennsylvania constitution. It reconvened on August 9, 1790. With minimal changes, the draft was accepted. The State constitution was ultimately ratified and signed into legislation. Lewis had been a successful driving force for change at state level. The Conservatives had won back their second legislative house and created a strong governorship.

In the midst of his work in the Pennsylvania General Assembly, Lewis was appointed the first United States Attorney for the District of Pennsylvania. As the first individual to hold this office, Lewis was officially appointed by President George Washington on September 26, 1789, just five months into his presidency.

On November 16, Lewis was officially sworn into court by Sam Caldwell, the clerk of the District Court:

> At a District-Court of the United States, held in Philadelphia, in and for the District of Pennsylvania, November Session 1789. William Lewis Esquire, was admitted an Attorney of the said District-Court, and took the Affirmation of Office. In testimony whereof I have hereunto subscribed my Name and affixed the Seal of

the said Court, this sixteenth Day of November, one thousand seven hundred and eighty-nine.[112]

Lewis's work as the United States Attorney for the District of Pennsylvania would be considered modest by modern standards—his caseload consisting of no more than a few dozen in the two years he would hold the office.

Yet another significant matter before the Pennsylvania General Assembly in 1789 was the issue of the charter of the College of Philadelphia. The college, originally called an "academy" and founded by Benjamin Franklin, had been given a charter in 1755. In 1779 the revolutionary legislature revoked the charter because of their belief that the school's provost, the Reverend William Smith, was a Loyalist. At the same time, they created the University of the State of Pennsylvania. Despite the loss of the charter, Smith, along with the remnants of the old board of trustees, continued to operate an attenuated version of the college while persisting in their efforts to regain control of the college property. William Lewis used his powers of persuasion to help the college, successfully convincing his fellow assemblymen to reinstate its original charters. Faculty members and trustees were also asked to return to their former posts with the school—Rush, Wistar, and Wilson took their places among the faculty once again. William Lewis was asked to fill one of several vacancies that remained on the board. He readily joined his fellow trustees, including William Bingham, Caspar Wistar, Henry Hill, Robert Hare, and Richard Peters—all very prominent men.[113] Benjamin Franklin was named the president of the college. The existence of two institutions of higher learning, each with its own campus and faculties, quickly led to serious administrative and financial problems for both. Two years later, in 1791, the General Assembly would vote to create a new charter that would join the two schools together to form the University of Pennsylvania. Each institution chose twelve men to serve a newly constituted board. At this time, Lewis became a trustee for the newly formed university. He would serve in this capacity for twenty-eight years, until his death.

On July 9, 1790, Philadelphia became the nation's capitol—a position it would hold for ten years. Federal offices were moved to or set up in Philadelphia during this period. One such entity was the United States Supreme Court. Established in New York City the year prior, the court had admitted twenty-seven "counselors" to the bar during its first session, with the requirements that applicants had to have practiced for three years or more in the supreme courts of their respective states of residence; had to have maintained a "fair . . . private and professional Character" during that time; and had to submit documentation proving they met these requirements.[114] Elias Boudinot, a leading colonial lawyer in New Jersey, became the first member of the United States Supreme Court bar in February 1790.

When the Supreme Court held its first term in Philadelphia in February 1791, a large number of lawyers appeared for admission to the bar, most without the required documentation in hand. Edward Burd, the prothonotary of the Supreme Court of Pennsylvania, was able to immediately supply certificates for twenty-two of the applicants who stated that they had practiced in Pennsylvania's highest courts. But the applicants still needed to prove their "good Moral Character and good legal Abilities." Only six of these twenty-two were admitted that first day, of whom William Lewis was the first; evidently, his reputation and experience was such that he did not need to prove anything further for admittance.[115] Within the month, the court turned to the Attorney General of the United States, Edmund Randolph, to arbitrate an individual's worthiness for admission. The first criminal proceedings of the U.S. Supreme

Court in 1791 consisted of four cases: two assaults, one murder, and one larceny on the high seas. The only case Lewis initiated was *U.S. v. Nobel & Steveson*, the murder case.[116]

The United States Supreme Court did not have its own court building in Philadelphia, so it was loaned space. The justices first convened in the Pennsylvania State House (Independence Hall), but by August 1791 the court had moved to the east wing of City Hall located next door.[117] The United States Supreme Court, however, was required to yield to the schedules of the other courts also meeting in this location, which included the Supreme Court of the State of Pennsylvania, the United States District Court of Pennsylvania, and the Court of the City of Philadelphia. The United States Supreme Court was scheduled to meet in Philadelphia twice a year, but the four justices required for an official session were not always available. Sometimes no session could be held. No one seemed to mind all that much, because there were so few cases in the beginning. Over the next ten years, the United States Supreme Court averaged seven cases a year.

In 1791 William Lewis was appointed by President Washington to become judge of the United States District Court of Pennsylvania. Lewis would replace Washington's first appointee, Francis Hopkinson, who had died suddenly in May. Lewis was an obvious choice—but he was quite reluctant to take on a lifetime appointment, initially refusing the President's request:

> Phila July 8th 1791
> Sir,
>
> I am honored with a communication very grateful to my feelings which you have been pleased to make to me through Major Jackson and under the impressions which it has occasioned I am truly sorry that circumstances oblige me to decline the proposed appointment.
>
> Altho it would be wrong in me to trouble you with many observations on the subject the respect which I at all times feel for you calls upon me to mention that being in a very eligible situation at the Bar in pursuit of Emolument as well as respectability of Employment and of an age perhaps best suited for it the meditated change would hardly be consistent with the duty which I owe to my family.[118]
>
> I have the honor to be with esteem
> your Excellencies Hml: Obt

This letter to the President was found among Lewis's estate papers, leaving the family to speculate that it was a draft, never sent, or perhaps that it had been returned to Lewis. Washington's personal secretary, Major William Jackson, likely the first to receive and read Lewis's response—and anticipating the reaction of the President—could have returned the letter to Lewis and personally implored him to reconsider. Lewis and Jackson were close friends. After his military career, Jackson had settled in Philadelphia and eventually studied law with Lewis. He was asked to be Washington's secretary the same year he had been admitted to the Court of Common Pleas and the Pennsylvania Supreme Court bar. Having been Lewis's pupil himself, Jackson would have known the best argument to present in hopes of changing his mind. Lewis would indeed acquiesce to the wishes of the president, but with the proviso that he would merely serve until another replacement could be found and no longer. Thomas Jefferson sent Lewis a letter on July 14 confirming this appointment:

Sir,

The President of the United States desiring to avail the Public of your services as Judge of the District Court in and for Pennsylvania District; I have now the Honor of enclosing you the Commission, and of expressing to you the sentiments of perfect esteem with which I am, Sir Your most obedient & most humble Servant

/s/ Th. Jefferson[119]

Jefferson also enclosed Lewis's commission from President Washington:

George Washington[,] President of the United States of America
To all who shall see these presents—Greeting
Whereas the Office of Judge of the District Court in and for Pennsylvania District is at present vacant,—
Know ye, that reposing special Trust and Confidence in the Wisdom, Uprightness and Learning of William Lewis of Pennsylvania, esquire, I do appoint him Judge of the District Court, and do authorize and empower him to execute and fulfill the Duties of that Office, according to the Constitution and Laws of the said United States; and to have and to hold the said Office, with all the Powers, Privileges and Emoluments to the same of Right appertaining unto him the said William Lewis, during his good behavior, and *until the end of the next session of the Senate of the United States, and no longer.*
In testimony whereof I have caused these letters to be made patent, and the Seal of the United States to be hereunto affixed. Given under my hand the fourteenth day of July in the Year of our Lord one thousand seven hundred and ninety-one, and of the Independence of the United States of America the sixteenth.

/s/ G. Washington

Lewis's terms for accepting this position are clearly stated in the commission. Lewis would do as he was asked, but the term would only be for about seven months. Lewis understood well what he would be giving up professionally in becoming a judge as he outlined in a letter to C. M. Randolph of the District Court at this time. The letter was meant to convey Lewis's sense of propriety and to acknowledge that he had taken steps to prevent conflicts of interest by declining to provide counsel or practice law. His stated exception, however, was that he would continue his practice in those cases which took place in the United States Supreme Court.

Two days later, Lewis appeared before his old friend James Wilson, who served as an associate judge of the Supreme Court of the United States, where he was sworn into office as attested to in the document signed by Wilson:

On the 16th Day of July 1791. Before me James Wilson Esquire one of the Judges of the Supreme Court of the United States appeared William Lewis Esquire Judge of the District Court for the Pennsylvania District and solemnly affirmed that he will support the Constitution of the United States; and also that he will administer justice without respect to Persons and do equal right to the poor and to the rich and that he

34

will faithfully and impartially discharge and perform all the duties incumbent on him as Judge of the District Court in and for the Pennsylvania District, according to the best of his abilities and understanding, agreeably to the Constitution and Laws of the United States

/s/ James Wilson[120]

William Lewis sent the following confirmation to Thomas Jefferson:

Philada. 17th July, 1791
Sir,

Permit me to acknowledge the receipt of the Commission which you have politely communicated to me from the President of the United States, appointing me Judge of the District Court of the Pennsylvania District and to declare my acceptance of that appointment. If it will not be giving you too much trouble I must beg you to make known to the President my respectful acknowledgments on this occasion with an assurance that my best endeavours shall not be wanting to merit the confidence which he has been pleased to repose in me

I am with sentiments of perfect regard
Your most obedient and most humble
Servant
/s/ Wm. Lewis[121]

Esther Ann McFarland, George C. McFarland, Jr., and the Honorable Thomas N. O'Neill, Jr., June 25, 2008 (portrait presentation, United States Courthouse, Philadelphia). Photo by Fred Pfaff.

During his stay on the bench, the federal courts were chiefly occupied with questions concerning their admiralty jurisdiction, as well as questions arising in the post-Revolutionary War period, such as expatriation and taxation. Upon completion of his term, President Washington attempted to reappoint Lewis for a full term as judge. Lewis held his ground this time. His friend William Rawle was approached to take on the judgeship, but he also declined. Rawle noted the following in his journal on the third of January 1792:

> Mr. Lewis having this day resigned the office of Judge of the District Court of Pennsylvania it was, by order of the President, offered to me.
> Considering my time of life, my increasing family, my emoluments and prospect at the bar I thought fit to decline it.[122]
> Lewis and Rawle's neighbor Richard Peters would be appointed to the position in the spring of 1792.

Lewis would continue to play a central role in advancing the Federalist platform over the next several years. While maintaining his office at "Fort Wilson" at Third and Walnut streets, Lewis found the federal government now operating at his doorstep—giving him ample opportunity to progress his opinions and to apply his knowledge at this critical time in the nation's development. His reputation was such that Lewis was often sought out for advice and counsel.

Lewis's knowledge of the law and his ability to successfully debate and communicate his opinions led both Thomas Jefferson, the nation's first secretary of state, and Alexander Hamilton, the nation's first secretary of the treasury, to seek his counsel. Jefferson and Hamilton were at the epicenter of the widening chasm between the emerging ideals of Republicanism and Federalism. During the first session of the first Congress in 1790, Hamilton would present his "First Report on the Public Credit" that would have the federal government assume state debts incurred during the Revolution. This would, in effect, give the federal government much more power by placing the country's most serious financial obligation in the hands of the federal, rather than the state, governments. Hamilton's plan was severely criticized by Jefferson, as he felt it passed beyond the scope of the new Constitutional government. However, after much debate Hamilton's resolution became law and met with immediate success.

By 1791, in order to continue to advance his Treasury Department initiatives, Hamilton made a recommendation that included three initiatives: to establish a National Mint to regulate coinage, to charter a National Bank of the United States, and to increase the excise tax on imported and domestic spirits to help fund the bank. A mint would allow for one "national" form of currency to replace the multiple state currencies utilized up to this point. The "bank bill" made it through the Senate, and, despite a day-long opposition speech from James Madison, it also passed through the House. Madison's main objection was that the Constitution did not provide the federal government with the authority to incorporate a bank. It would be up to the President to sign the bill into law. He was perplexed, however, as he believed that the principal function of the presidential veto was to protect the Constitution.[123] Washington called Madison in for a conference and asked the advice of Jefferson and other cabinet members. The developing debate was a confrontation between two basic attitudes toward the Constitution: "strict interpretation" (Republicans) versus "implied powers" (Federalists).

Hamilton, caught off guard by Madison's stance—an about-face from the man who had helped write the Federalist papers—worked feverishly for days on a rebuttal to be submitted to Washington. To ensure that all of Madison's objections were properly addressed, Hamilton sought the advice of William Lewis, his friend and neighbor, who served as an unofficial advisor throughout his career.[124] Who better than Lewis to discern the strong and weak points in the defense of an argument?

Lewis had a great respect for Hamilton. He liked to tell a story of a particular trial in New York at which Lewis was representing one of the parties. When the trial was about to start, the opposing counsel fell ill. Lewis was asked to update the stand-in counsel, Alexander Hamilton, to whom he provided a detailed statement of his case. Lewis recounted:

> he thanked me, left me, and in an hour afterward we met in court and the argument at once proceeded. I spoke for several hours. The judges seemed convinced and I was perfectly satisfied with them and myself. During the argument Mr. Hamilton took no notes, sometimes fixed his penetrating eyes upon me, and sometimes walked the chamber, apparently deeply interested, but exhibiting no anxiety. When I finished he took the floor, and, to my amazement, he acknowledged all my points and denied none of my authorities, but assumed a position which had never entered my mind, to the support of which directing all his great powers, in one-fourth of the time employed by me, he not only satisfied the court, but convinced me that I was utterly wrong. In short, after my time and toil and confidence, I was beaten, shamefully beaten.[125]

In the case of Hamilton's rebuttal to Madison, his response to Washington pointed out that "strict interpretation" would, by banning any response to new situations, soon make the federal government obsolete. The state governments, being not similarly tied, would keep up to date and therefore take over, defeating the object of the federal union. This argument was, as most modern historians agree, unanswerable.[126] President Washington had no choice but to sign the bill; on April 25, 1791, the bank bill became law. The United States would not model their currency after the British pound but would create a currency based on the Spanish dollar. Horace Binney wrote that Lewis was quite proud of his advisory role and the fact that Hamilton was able to convince Washington not to veto the bank bill. His pride had less to do with the bill however, and more to do with the fact that Hamilton, in Binney's words, "prostrated, for the time, the political metaphysics of Mr. Jefferson" and his Republican ideals.[127]

 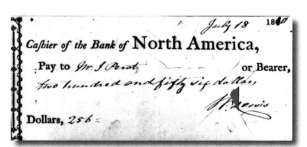

North American Bank checks. Lewis family papers.

Despite the difference in their political views, correspondence from Thomas Jefferson shows that he too looked to Lewis for guidance, specifically on the topic of British debts during the Revolution. Jefferson and Lewis seem to have been of the same opinion on the topic of British debt; in a letter to a Mr. Hammond, Jefferson actually cites Lewis's opinion in support of his own views.[128] In further correspondence sent to Lewis, Jefferson made clear his appreciation, not just for Lewis's expertise, but for his willingness to help instruct and prepare his political opponent:

> The recess of Congress permits me now to resume the subject of my letter of August 12 and to acknowledge the receipt of your previous of Sep. 1, Nov. 28 & Jan. 1 with respect to British debts and property it was thought possible then that they might come forward and dismiss the interest & questions existing between the two nations, and we know they would assail us on the subject of the treaty, without our previously knowing the particular state or states. Those proceedings they would make the ground of complaint, we wished to be in a state of preparation on every point. I am therefore to thank you particularly for having furnished us the justifications of this commonwealth in your letter of Jan.1. With respect to the more general object of my letter, that of working a very complete collection of all the laws in force or which were reinforce in the several states, we are now as to this state possessed of those from 1776 to 1790. I must still avail myself of your kind understanding in your letter of Sept. 12 or Nov. 28 to continue your attention to this [reparation?] 'till we can have the whole. Indeed if you would order any bond- seller to promise them according to each list as you have given him, it might greatly lessen your trouble, & he would deliver them himself at my office & [sessions?] these his [pay?] Whenever you shall be as good as to notify me of the rest of those already from wished it shall be immediately reimbursed. I am sure you are sensible of the comforts of justifying at the rest of the general comment a complete collection of all the laws of all the states & hope you will perceive these more as persons as likely to make the collection judiciously as the previous for the [illegible], what must be the apology for the trouble which has been given on this subject by him who has the honor to be with great esteem & respect his
>
> Your most reverent & most humble servant[129]

When Jefferson wrote to Lewis on April, 5, 1791, to arrange for a collection of case laws to be transcribed and indexed with Lewis's assistance, he confessed, "It is with some degree of shame that I accept the kind offer."[130]

In the coming months, Lewis would turn his attention to the elections of 1792—both state and federal—and the increasing debate between the emergent Federalists and Republicans. The two groups did share several common aims: a profound respect for the sanctity of property, the need for a stable representative government, and the wish to uphold both the state and national constitutions. And while the upcoming elections held no burning issues to spark statewide discussions or to mold public opinion—nor had either group yet created organizational structures that would allow for inclusion of statewide input—the contest, its procedures, and its eventual outcome would have lasting effects on both groups. The contest of 1792 would be born of a curious mixture of divergent nomination procedures, old political feuds and resentments, and personal rivalries and ambitions. And, as it turned out, neither group would be sufficiently strong or confident enough to present two distinct congressional tickets to the public.

Simply put, when Pennsylvania's new state constitution was adopted in September 1790, it provided no satisfactory means to nominate federal representatives or presidential electors (in the 1792 cycle). The confusion over how such nominations should be obtained would ultimately create a more pronounced political split.[131] General election laws were passed to help correct the initial oversight in the state constitution, but these same laws forced the politicians to devise some sort of statewide nomination machinery. This would be the root of much turmoil to come.[132]

The work of creating election tickets was done by a small coterie of Philadelphia insiders whose particular affiliations might mean little to an "outsider" across the state. Distinctions among the factions were always in a state of flux and they held numerous and confusing labels. This was especially true in Pennsylvania, where state issues tended to be conflated with federal issues, particularly when the federal government moved to Philadelphia. Those individuals who wanted a strong national government and who had advocated for a strong federal constitution were now being called Federalists, but had been known formerly in Pennsylvania as Conservatives and Anti-Constitutionalists. The emerging Republicans, who feared federal power, were often still referred to as Constitutionalists. And while there was always the assumption that the Federalists lived in the more urban, eastern part of Pennsylvania and that the Republicans lived in the western counties, strong pockets of both factions could actually be found in both locations.[133]

One particular gathering of these Philadelphia insiders on July 19, 1792—a group that was preponderantly Federalist in sentiment—led to a series of escalating meetings which would include members of both factions working to "outdo" and "undo" the work of the other's sessions. Members of the group met at the State House to promote their idea of holding a statewide conference in which they planned to obtain opinions on which persons should be nominated for candidacy to federal office. The initial meeting was sparsely attended but did include several individuals who opposed this idea of a conference to select candidates.[134] On the July 25, the group met again. They elected Philadelphia Mayor Matthew Clarkson as chairman, and then a motion was made to create a ward committee, which would then propose names for a Committee of Correspondence and a Committee of Conference. This motion led to a heated discussion, and as the hour grew late the group adjourned with a plan to meet two days later. The next meeting, held on July 27, only made things worse. Those opposed to the idea of a conference—a preponderantly Republican group led by Alexander Dallas and Dr. Hutchinson, moved to have the records of the previous meetings expunged. This motion was defeated, and the group adjourned without coming to a consensus as to whether conferees should be appointed.

With no date set for a future meeting, the Dallas-Hutchinson group called a meeting of its own, advertising in the local papers that it would convene at seven o'clock in the evening, when the day's work was done—a pointed tactic to attract a large group of pro-Republican tradesmen.[135] When the citizens arrived at the State House on July 30, it was found that the assembly room was much too small to accommodate the crowd, so they all headed out to the yard. As the meeting began, Hutchinson arose to review the events of the past meeting and to make it clear that he strongly opposed a state convention to select Congressional candidates. A motion to expunge the records from the previous meeting passed when it was decided that more men were in opposition to the idea of holding a conference than were for it (as the previous meeting minutes had indicated.) A second successful motion was passed that required the appointment of a seven-man Committee of Correspondence, the duty of which would be to determine the opinion of the electors throughout the state. At this point, after four meetings had been held to determine a nominating procedure, it came down to Conferees (generally Federalists) versus Correspondents (generally Republican).

Despite the positive vote for the appointment of the Committee of Correspondence, the Conferees—many of whom had boycotted the meeting on the 30th—had already notified the citizens of Philadelphia through several local newspapers that their group would meet at three o'clock the following afternoon. The Correspondents, unwilling to let their opponents hold a meeting without opposition, quickly decided to convene a meeting at the same time and place. The quarrel between the two factions had now officially become public, and the stage was set for mayhem.

Both factions started their meetings independently of the other, both in the State House yard, with a crowd milling about the proceedings. Wild shouting of yeas and nays from the assemblage created one big scene of confusion. While the Conferees attempted to move their group away to the western side of the yard, their table and chair were seized by the mob and torn to pieces. More severe violence was prevented with difficulty.[136] As the hours progressed, the number of men in favor of the correspondence scheme seemed to increase, to the point that the Conferees became discouraged and finally left the yard.

The Conferees gave up attempts to hold any more general meetings in Philadelphia; instead they started to meet behind closed doors with a smaller contingent of supporters. The group met the first week in August at Epple's Tavern, where they appointed a committee to correspond with the rest of the state. The committee of nine included George Latimer, Robert Waln, William Lewis, Israel Whelen, William Rawle, Richard Wells, Hilary Baker, John Wilcocks, and Benjamin R. Morgan. Both the Conferees and the Correspondents published circulars explaining the recent events along with their pleas for support, basically ignoring the activities of the other.

The battle then moved to the local papers. On October 9, 1792, one particular broadside made the charge that a select few Conferees were attempting to usurp the right of popular selection by claiming that privilege themselves. William Lewis, known publicly as a leader of the Conferees, was considered to be the principal offender.[137] Still another writer pointed out that *both* groups had hatched secret plots, and that both were led by "aristocrats" who were "equally enemies of the Commonwealth." The citizens were encouraged to "be free and independent" and vote as they wished. Republicans continued to disparage the Federalists by referring to them as "aristocrats," and the Federalists returned the favor by calling the Republicans "Anti-Federalists."

The Correspondents officially published their list of candidates, which, they claimed, had been winnowed down from the hundreds of names they had received from across the state. The ticket, published as the "Rights of Man Ticket," was identical to the list that the Republicans had talked about much earlier. Discussion continued in the newspapers. A Federalist response from a man writing under the pseudonym "Cerberus" printed an exposé in the *General Advertiser* accusing the Correspondents of having prepared their electors list much earlier in private, despite their claims of reaching out to the tradesman and the public at large. Upon being challenged, "Cerberus" printed a copy of a letter sent from Ebenezer Bowman to William Lewis on August 5 in which Bowman had enclosed the exact list of eleven candidates that had been published in late September.

The Federalists continued to hold meetings and gather names, and at last they held their electors convention in Lancaster on September 20, 1792. Only nine counties actually showed up to be represented. At the close of the conference, the Federalists published their ticket.

After all the shenanigans and maneuvering, it was found that of the thirteen congressional candidates listed on each factions' ticket, the names of seven men appeared on both tickets—regardless of their political tendencies. The individuals too popular to be excluded by either side were William Findley, Frederick A. Muhlenberg, Daniel Hiester, William Irvine, Peter Muhlenberg, Thomas Hartley, and John W. Kittera. Hiester and both Muhlenbergs were deemed essential to win the large German vote. In the end, the congressional contest would come down to the six individuals above and beyond the seven in common.

Both sides hoped to elect their entire slate of thirteen candidates, but when the votes were counted on Election Day (October 9), the votes had been split. The seven common candidates were easily elected, along with James Armstrong, Thomas Fitzsimmons, and Thomas Scott for the Federalists and Andrew Gregg, William Montgomery, and John Smilie for the Republicans. It should be noted that in comparison, the electors for the presidential race were a foregone conclusion, as no one would seriously contest Washington's reelection.

Lewis led the charge to get Federalists voted in to represent Pennsylvania in the United States Congress—he himself had been urged to run for the United States Congress, but had declined, as he didn't really want to hold an elected office.[138] At the same time, he was also deeply involved in the state elections, which were taking place concurrently. The Pennsylvania 1792 legislature elections are not often discussed, as they have been mostly overshadowed by the tomfoolery of the federal election proceedings, but this particular election would have major repercussions for the Federalist Party.

Just as the leaders of the opposing parties had placed the same names on their congressional ballots, they did the same thing for the Pennsylvania State Assembly election. Of the five candidates listed for the Pennsylvania General Assembly, the same four names appeared on both ballots. The election would come down to a contest for the fifth spot only.[139]

Lewis was very much involved in putting together tickets for this election. On October 1, 1790, a gathering of likeminded folks (Pennsylvania Conservatives and future Federalists) nominated five persons for the State House, including John D. Coxe. Four days later, Coxe announced his retirement from the House—something that was not unusual at the time. The group met again and unanimously inserted William Lewis for Coxe. As one of the driving forces behind the Federalist Party in Philadelphia, Lewis was an easy call, despite the fact that he had not intended to run for reelection to the General Assembly, having already served two terms. The opposition pitted John Swanwick against Lewis in the fifth slot. Swanwick was a politically ambitious merchant who had enjoyed a swift rise to fame in the commercial world. That his financial success had not brought him into the inner circle of Philadelphia's social elite, and that he objected to the Washington administration's pro-British commercial and revenue policies, put him decidedly in the Republican camp, despite his earlier Conservative leanings. He now envisioned a "new, liberal economic order being created in America, one that would be run by a 'natural aristocracy' and a 'new commercial order.'"[140]

The state General Assembly contest with four identical names on each ticket would therefore boil down to Swanwick versus Lewis. Perhaps Swanwick benefited from the extreme actions the Republicans (Correspondents) were taking for the Federal congressional election, as they had worked diligently pushing the "Rights of Man" ticket. The Republicans had openly campaigned against Lewis, calling attention to what they called the "consummate display of presumption and boldness of the Aristocratic junto." One pro-Republican newspaper attacked Lewis, publicly naming him as the leader of the Conferees in the congressional race, which may well have affected voters' opinions. In such a heated contest, Lewis was an easy target. Still, Lewis had his supporters as well. On October 9, 1792, the Federal Gazette published the following open letter to William Lewis:

> To Wm. Lewis, Esquire.
> Sir,
> The sacrifice you have made in consenting to serve your fellow citizens once more in the Legislature of this State, excites in our bosoms the warmest sentiments of gratitude—We know you resolutely declined every overture which was made to you to stand as a candidate for Representative to Congress. If it was honor you sought, there indeed, was an ample field for your eminent abilities to have display—your fellow-citizens lamented your refusal to gratify their wishes; but knowing the importance of your active rank at the bar, they could not become importunate. How much then are we indebted to you for your consenting to fill a humbler station in our State Legislature—a station which will demand more of your valuable time—your country cannot forget this memorable sacrifice, and surely there is not a good citizen amongst us who will not heartily unite with those who solicited your name, in placing you amongst our Representatives.
> That you may feel much less of the inconveniences of the appointment than your apprehensions have suggested is the honest wish of
>
> MANY THOUSANDS[141]

Ultimately, when the votes were counted, Swanwick defeated Lewis by the narrow margin of sixty-five votes. This was the first setback the Federalists had suffered since the establishment of the new government.[142]

A perfect storm of overseas political events would further cement the growing political divide between the Federalists and the Democratic-Republicans. First, in January 1793 the Americans would learn that French revolutionaries guillotined King Louis XVI. His queen, Marie Antoinette, would be beheaded in October of 1793, while their son, the Dauphin, would eventually die while imprisoned. During France's Reign of Terror thousands of people accused of being antirevolutionary would face the guillotine. France declared war on Great Britain and the Netherlands. The Republicans in America remained strong Francophiles and supported the Reign of Terror—especially those, such as the Marquis de Lafayette, who had helped the States achieve independence. Further, they denounced Hamilton, Adams, and even Washington as friends of Britain, proclaiming them secret monarchists and enemies of the republican values. The trouble between France and England would further complicate the foreign policy decisions being debated by the Washington administration—and would do so for many years to come.

At home in Philadelphia, the outbreak of yellow fever would not only bring the city to its proverbial knees at its height in October of 1793, but it would also bring the debate between the Democratic-Republicans and the Federalists into even sharper focus. The yellow fever had a direct impact on politics, not least of which was the loss of several key political players who had died during the epidemic; two of note were Federalist Samuel Powel, the former mayor and general assemblyman, and Republican Dr. Hutchinson, who had played a key role in leading the Rights of Man contingent during the elections two years prior.

The Republicans took full political advantage of the circumstances surrounding the epidemic as one of their own, Stephan Girard, became a hero during this time. Before the outbreak, most of the doctors in town were considered avid Federalists. A good number of these doctors—like everyone else with the means to do so—left town at the onset of the yellow fever. Of those who remained, ten died and several worked while stricken with fever, including the famous Dr. Benjamin Rush. With medical services sorely lacking, Stephen Girard—a Frenchman who had made his fortunes in shipping—set up and financed the Bush Hill hospital, which he staffed with specialists brought in from the Caribbean. Girard's background and experience put him in firm opposition to what he viewed as the pro-British trade policies of the Washington administration. That the Bush Hill hospital came to the aid of the artisans, tradesmen, servants, and slaves who were left to their own devices did not go unnoticed by the underclasses; the Republicans were seen as saviors while the Federalists left town. Even Dr. Rush, Lewis's good friend and neighbor, started to associate himself more strongly with the Republicans.

When the Federalists returned to town and the Third Congress was finally able to convene in December 1793, the Republicans found they had returned ready for a fight. Albert Gallatin had come to town to take the oath of office to join the United States Senate. That same day, however, nineteen Pennsylvania Federalists, represented by William Lewis, filed a protest with the Senate stating that Gallatin did not have the minimum nine years of citizenship required to hold office as a senator. Gallatin was a devoted Anti-Federalist and native of Switzerland who had settled in the western Pennsylvania county of Fayette, where he had served as a representative in the state legislature. He was also a vocal opponent of Hamilton's financial plans. Lewis would bring to light Gallatin's calculation of his years as a United States citizen—which in Lewis's view was only eight years.[143]

Up to this point the U.S. Senate sessions had been closed to the public, but on this occasion the senate chamber was opened, as the Senators hoped to prove their egalitarian attitude. Additionally, this would be the first time a professional counselor would represent petitioners in the Senate. William Lewis, the Federalist representative of the petitioners, would officially go on record as the first counselor to appear before the United States Senate.[144]

Lewis's petition was sent to a Senate committee, which duly reported that Gallatin indeed had not been a citizen for the required number of years. Gallatin rebutted the report, noting his unbroken residence of thirteen years in the United States, his 1785 oath of allegiance to the Commonwealth of Virginia, his substantial property holdings, and, most important, his years of service in the Pennsylvania legislature.[145] A second review committee recommended Gallatin's removal. Two months later, on February 28, 1794, the Senate voted fourteen to twelve in favor of Gallatin's dismissal. The vote was split along the Federalist and Republican Party lines. Despite his short time in the Senate, Gallatin gained popularity as an effective opponent of Hamilton. This election controversy provided him even further notoriety as he was duly elected to the House of Representatives the following session.

John Swanwick, Lewis's nemesis from the 1792 Pennsylvania General Assembly elections, would come back on the political scene to take advantage of the prevailing climate. He decided to run for United States Congress as the Pennsylvania Democratic-Republican candidate during the 1794 election cycle. His opponent was the incumbent Thomas Fitzsimmons, a well-heeled, Federalist Philadelphian who had helped found the Bank of North America. With the help of improved organization across Pennsylvania, the Republicans increased their voter participation by 4 percent from two years previous to a total of 34 percent. Swanwick was able to carry the day with slightly more than 51 percent of the vote.[146] Swanwick's win was helped by an aggressive "common man" campaign, which had greatly increased his appeal to the general public.

The presidential election of 1796 would prove to be a key turning point in the rise of Republicanism. While the Federalists maintained control, with John Adams elected the first Federalist president, the Republican Thomas Jefferson came in second place and would become vice president. When Jefferson became president four years later, the federal government looked much different than it did twelve years prior. When George Washington took office as president with John Adams as his vice president, the United States had two executive officers. Jefferson would inherit a federal administration that included three thousand civilian employees and a substantial military force, supplemented by a significant number of private contractors. The Washington administration—with strong Federalist backing—had moved forcefully to establish the departments of Treasury, State, and War. More specifically, they worked to nationalize responsibility for the Revolutionary War debts, to establish a national bank and a sound financial currency, to institute an effective system of taxation, and to create a national court system. The Washington administration also believed that national security depended on a strong army and navy. When Jefferson assumed the presidency, the crisis in France had passed. He slashed army and navy expenditures, cut the budget, and eliminated the tax on whiskey. He was able to slash the national debt by one-third.[147] With a Republican administration now in place, the major Federalist role after 1800 would come in the judiciary.

Federalists may have fallen out of favor by the time Jefferson was voted into office, but William Lewis had not lost interest in the ongoing transactions surrounding the federal elections. Not only had he not lost interest, but he was determined to reignite the Federalist cause. On September 21, 1805, The *United States' Gazette* published an address written by William Lewis to the federal electors of Pennsylvania, who would be deciding upon the candidates for the upcoming U.S. Senate and House of Representatives races. In it, Lewis challenged his fellow Federalists to awake from years of inactivity and to start acting as a single body once again. He hoped to discourage those Federalists who were considering forming a "third party" by uniting with the more moderate arm of the Democratic-Republicans. And while he had no inclination to believe that the Federalists would ever regain the power they once had, he believed the Federalist voice was as important as ever—even if only on an equal level of participation. Bottom line, Lewis urged all Federalists to step up and pursue office and encouraged the federal electors to plant the seeds by recommending such candidates. It wasn't just the Constitution at risk; "our country and all that is dear to us are at stake."

The printed address was preceded by an editorial from the paper's publisher:

It is with pleasure that we this day give publicity to the able address of WILLIAM

LEWIS, Esq. to the federal electors of Pennsylvania; and we assure that gentleman that we feel no disposition to avail ourselves of the privilege, which he has facetiously granted us, of *"basting it."* It is true that the editor of this Gazette feels no very lively individual interest in the event of the approaching election. He perceives in the front ranks of both the parties, which are now struggling for the supremacy, persons whose political characters he totally and almost equally reprobates, and his own opinion is, that a perfect neutrality on the part of the federalists, especially as it respects the office of governour in particular, would be the wisest policy. But he is by no means conscious of being bigotted *[sic]* in this opinion, and certainly feels no disposition to stigmatise those who think and act differently as deserters or apostates. Such being his sentiments and feelings, he will with perfect alacrity give publicity, to any temperate and well written articles which may be offered him upon the subject. If this Gazette has hitherto born the complexion of hostility to those federalists who are disposed, on this occasion, to unite with the friends of governour McKean, it has been because the writers who have espoused that cause have chosen other papers for the communication of their sentiments, and because the ablest essays which we have seen in the papers of the neighbouring states have been in opposition to such a union. The editor therefore explicitly declares that he shall feel gratified by the communication of the sentiments of his friends on both sides, and that his paper will be open alike to all who wish to express their opinions upon the course which the federalists either as a party or as individuals ought to pursue.[148]

§

Lewis's address:

TO THE FEDERAL ELECTORS OF PENNSYLVANIA.
Gentlemen,

The awful crisis has arrived, when an imperious duty demands, that we reflect on our situation, and coolly, but firmly, determine, on the part we should take at the approaching Election. The occasion is far from an ordinary one, and the event may be momentous to ourselves and posterity. It therefore behoves *[sic]* us to consider well before we resolve, & then to act as if our all were at stake. A listless indifference is seldom commendable—at present it is altogether inexcusable. We have held no meetings on the subject that I was privy to, and if individual sentiments are formed, they have not to my knowledge been generally communicated among us. Under these circumstances, it will not, I hope, be deemed assuming, in one of your number, whose former situations in life made him known to many of you, frankly to submit his thoughts to you, and then leave you to act, as reason, conscience, and love for your country may dictate.

While I supposed it best, for the wayward political opinions, that have long convulsed the commonwealth and menaced its dissolution, to be left to their mad career, and to spend themselves to their own folly, I remained a silent spectator of their progress without interfering in their direction. To this I was led from a real or supposed knowledge of human nature, which taught me to believe, that the when the rage and fury of the day, from whatever cause arising take their course, they will pursue it in spite of all the reason and argument that can be urged to prevent it, until they arrive at a certain point. That point attained, history and experience have shown, that the better part of the infatuated multitude, like *"intoxicated men stunned into sobriety,"* are apt to start at the precipice before them, and to shrink from the danger to which they had heedlessly run. That time seems to have fortunately come, and if it has, it must be the proper one, for all federalists to ponder well the situation of our country, and to rouse from their slumbers, with renewed strength, for its preservation. We should not suffer the years of inactivity which we have passed, to benumb our senses, but we should awake to vigilance, and more than our former exertions. That *"the commonwealth should never be despaired of,"* was a maxim of the ancient Romans, founded in patriotism and a genuine love of their country, and it is worthy of every man whose heart is not alien to the country in which, it beats. That you, to whom I address myself, have no such *alien* hearts, I well know; and that you will not suffer the commonwealth to perish, I firmly believe—BUT BY WHAT MEANS SHALL IT BE SAVED? On this interesting question I had hoped, that all federalists would think and act alike, and that we may do so, is the object of this address.

Some of you may perhaps think, a kind of *political amalgamation* necessary, and that we should unite in one body with the more moderate or better part of the democrats, who form what is called the *third party*; but if any of you are of this opinion, I hope the number is small. Federalism will admit of no *alloy*; and a dereliction of its fundamental truths in whole or in part, for the sake of office or power, or for any other temporising purpose, would be disgraceful to ourselves, and a degradation of the name that we bear. A spirit of conciliation is, I acknowledge, often commendable, but it can never be so, at the sacrifice of principles altogether correct, for others that are but partially so. It is therefore hoped, that no such union will be seriously thought of whatever temporary benefits it might promise to a few individuals. Besides if the name of FEDERALISM, is of such little estimation with any among us that they are willing to exchange it for another, and thereby belie the principles of our *great benefactors*, who honourably bore it when living, and left the fair inheritance at their deaths, to those who survived them,—I, for one, am not of that number.—Some others of you it is said are—but this may Heaven forefend! for uniting with the disorganizers in the call of a convention, and the destruction of the present order of things, in the idle hope of the promised *perfectability*. This is almost too incredible to be worth mentioning. If resentment exists in the minds of any or all of us, it may on proper occasions be excusable, and perhaps justifiable; but its exercise cannot be so, where it carries with it our own destruction, and that of *our country*. Large allowances should certainly be made for our feelings, but they should not be suffered to league us with the most frantick and ferocious enemies of our country, for the sake of destroying others, in a case too, where we must perish with them. If we do this, we are no federalists; but the blind and merciless victims of our own passions and we shall be as deservedly trampled in the dust, as the infatuated

Britons were by the Romans; or, as the Romans were by the Goths and Vandals.

Some others of you I believe think, that all federalists should stand aloof, and leave it to the democrats and disorganizers to fight out their own battles, that we may profit by their conflicts, and regain our former power and legitimate rights. This opinion might perhaps be correct, were there reasonable grounds to expect the event, which those politicians predict; but I fear they are mistaken, and that if their advice is followed, we shall be involved in one common ruin by the substitution of a *despotick anarchy*, bordering on Vandalism, in the place of liberty and order, law and regular governments, with their concomitant blessings. I do not mean to say, that *we federalists* are at present in the equal participation with others, of all these things, but our constitution entitles us to it, and if we are wise enough to preserve it from the hands of those, whose devoted victim it is, we shall one day enjoy our due proportion of them. This is all that can reasonably be expected from any constitution, and as every thing else depends on ourselves, we shall have much to answer for, to our country and posterity, if from lethargy on the one hand, or an ill timed resentment on the other, we do not exert our best endeavours, to avert the evils that await us. We should then consider, what conduct, on our part, promises to be most salutary.

You will judge for yourselves, but it appears to me, that *freely communicating together, and animating each other, in mutual exertion, we should devest ourselves at least for the present, of all personal and party resentments, of every minor consideration, to that of,* **Saving our Constitution from immediate Destruction**; And of SAVING IT FROM DESTRUCTION, NO LESS CERTAIN, BY SUFFERING IT TO FALL INTO THE HANDS OF ITS FRANTICK ENEMY *(SNYDER)* AND OF THE FOREIGN EMMISARIES WHO WILL GOVERN BOTH HIM AND US.

And that to effect this, we should one and all come forward as Federalists, unconnected with any other party, at the next general election, and vote for men (no matter what party they may be) to fill every elective station in government, who are steadily opposed to Jacobinism or Democracy run mad, and firmly attached to our Constitution, and Government of Laws.

This will be treading in the steps, and profiting by the precepts and examples of the great WASHINGTON and HAMILTON. It will be no dereliction of our political principles, but an adhering to them—no attaching ourselves to any party; but holding ourselves alike independent of them all—and it will leave to such of them, as are not wanting in grace, an opportunity to see the errour of their ways—to turn from them, and to cleave unto Federalism, as the rock of their political Salvation. It will do more; it will in all human probability, be the means of preserving to real Pennsylvanians, the right of *self government*, and of discarding in due time, the corrupt influence and overbearing sway of the discontented and profligate outcasts of Europe.

It may perhaps be objected by some—I hope not by many, that by pursuing the conduct which has been recommended, the machinations of Jacobinism may be defeated, and the power of the third party be prolonged; but that federalists will not be brought into office, nor to their just weight in government. This supposition is I believe true in fact, but the monstrous conclusion of those who make it seems to be, that unless they can get into office and power, the constitution, the law and the commonwealth may, for aught that they care, perish in one general wreck under the scourge of democratick fury. I do not suppose this to be the real sentiment of any one of you, but the inevitable consequence is the same, whatever the motive may be. This is by far the most painful part of the task that I have undertaken. That talents—integrity—a capacity for business and an attention to it, should be the principal recommendation for office is true, and it is equally true, that if they were *the recommendations, a larger* portion than at present of the offices, under this state and the United States, would be filled by federalists. But it is not the character of federalists to be hungry office hunters—nor should our political conduct be influenced by any considerations of the kind *when our country, and all that is dear to us are at stake*. I have now discharged my duty.—A highly important one remains to be performed by you. If it is not well done, you may mourn in sack-cloth and ashes, but Posterity will execrate your names.

I am,
Your friend and servant,
WILLIAM LEWIS.

Five

Useful Citizen:

Lewis Builds Foundations in the Country's Foremost City

Lewis's success as a lawyer and statesman depended in good part upon the network of friends and associates he created. While Philadelphia was a populous and important port city, in many ways it remained a very small town. The leading families—interconnected by marriage and commerce—maintained homes within a small radius of each other. Before the end of the Revolution, Lewis settled his family into a house on the southwest corner of Third and Walnut Streets. Formerly the home of the celebrated lawyer and Declaration signer James Wilson, the house (nicknamed "Fort Wilson") put Lewis in the center of the action. He was steps from Carpenters' Hall and two blocks from

Fort Wilson, corner of Third and Walnut Streets, watercolor by Benjamin Ridgway Evans. Historical Society of Pennsylvania.

the State House (later Independence Hall). A block east was the City Tavern, where one could find the city's most prominent citizens enjoying food or camaraderie. Across Walnut Street lived Bishop William White (rector of both Christ and St. Peter's Churches), who lived next door to the famous Dr.

49

William Lewis historic marker. Photo by Fred Pfaff.

Esther Ann McFarland and George C. McFarland, Jr., at the unveiling of the William Lewis historic marker at Third and Walnut Streets, c. 1976. Photo by Fred Pfaff.

Benjamin Rush; across Third Street lived Alexander Hamilton. Half a block south on Third Street lived Thomas Willing, Richard Peters, Samuel Powel, and William Bingham. Even George and Martha Washington lived a few doors away until they moved into the newly renovated President's House.

The bonds formed at the corner of Third and Walnut would have a lasting impact on Lewis's career and his politics—his friendships with Alexander Hamilton and Benjamin Rush most especially. William Rawle, also a Third Street neighbor, would become another important friend to Lewis. It is through Rawle's personal journals that we have some understanding of Lewis's associations and social life. One particular entry notes that Lewis had been invited to dinner at Alexander Wilcock's on June 16, 1786 (although he was "engaged or left town" before the invitation had arrived).[149] Others invited included Tench Coxe, Major Jackson, Tilgham, Rush, and Shippen. A few days later Rawle noted, "Ingersoll, Lewis and myself staid to supper" in reference to a later visit to Wilcock's house. Guests included Wilcock's brother-in-law Benjamin Chew, Jr., socialite Henrietta Chew, Thomas Mifflin (later governor), and businessman John Swanwick. Social events such as these would have provided plenty of opportunity to discuss politics, especially later in the evening, as Rawle indicates that Wilcocks, Ingersoll, Rawle, and Lewis—unquestionably the leading lawyers in the city at that time, attended the supper.

Philadelphia would gain a reputation as one of the most beautiful cities in the world; it featured William Penn's public squares and the neoclassical architecture of grand public buildings such as the State House and Congress Hall. It was home to learned societies such as the American Philosophical Society and the Public Library as well as to coffeehouses and hundreds of taverns. The city stretched north and south from Vine Street to South Street and east and west from the Delaware River to Fifth Street. Beyond Twelfth Street one could find open pasture. Penn's "holy experiment" had attracted people of many races and religions—including a large population of

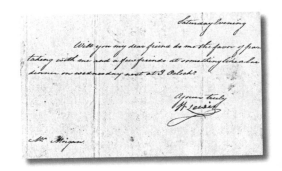

William Lewis to Dr. John Morgan. Lewis family papers.

free African Americans—to Philadelphia, creating a population of diverse nationalities and beliefs. With more than 42,000 citizens by the start of the Revolution, Philadelphia would grow to well over 55,000 people by the time it became the nation's capitol. The city and its diverse inhabitants would certainly help to determine what it meant to be a citizen of this newly emerging nation.

How odd it would have been for William Lewis and James Wilson as they worked so diligently in defense of those accused of treason during this period to hear of the treachery of Benedict Arnold in September of 1780. Lewis and Wilson were well acquainted with Arnold, not just as the military governor of Philadelphia appointed after the British evacuated, but as their client in the Olmstead case. They all had attended the grand parties hosted by the Binghams and the Powels at which Arnold had met debutant Margaret Peggy Shippen. Before Arnold was relocated to a new post, he had married Peggy and purchased Mount Pleasant with plans to renovate it and install his new bride in a glamorous country estate upon his return. The scandal, rife with intrigue, was discussed throughout the city. Despite their social connections, the Shippen family was known to be Loyalist, and Peggy had had a rumored relationship with Major John André the British officer who was captured while traveling with the papers outlining Arnold's plot while he had been stationed in the city during the British occupation. Philadelphians were angry and moved to demonstrate against Arnold. The artist Charles Willson Peale created an effigy an elaborate float portraying a Janus-faced Arnold, accompanied by the devil, who stood behind Arnold in a long black robe, shaking a money bag in one hand and a pitchfork in the other. As darkness fell on September 30, the float moved slowly up and down the streets of Philadelphia, accompanied by fifes and drums playing the rogue's march, the cavalry of the city troop, a company of militia men marching with lighted candles in their muzzles, and a troop of boys carrying candles. Hour after hour they marched through the streets until at last they arrived at High Street (Market) and the Delaware River, where the effigy was set ablaze.[150]

This sort of demonstration, often a celebration, was much enjoyed by the citizens of Philadelphia. Whether the occasion was a downfall, a conquest, or a surrender, there were floats, dances, fireworks, house decorations, and all manner of displays to behold. Philadelphians would celebrate the surrender of British General Lord Cornwallis at Yorktown in October 1781, the triumphant arrival of General George Washington in November of 1781, and in support of the war hero Marquis de Lafayette and his fellow Frenchmen, they would embrace *la joie de vivre* and celebrate the birth of the French dauphin in May 1782 and the birthday of Louis XVI in August of 1782. They would celebrate on April 16, 1783, when Sheriff William Will announced that hostilities between Great Britain and America had come to an end, and on September 30, 1783, when the Treaty of Paris was signed. Before the official exchange of ratified documents in May of 1784, Philadelphians planned the ultimate celebration in January 1784. Revelers crowded the streets to view oversized illuminated displays and came together at Sixth and Market Streets, where Peale had built his elaborate Triumphal Arch. Measuring 56.5 feet wide and 40 feet tall, the arch featured a gigantic figure of Peace, attended by goddesses, descending from its top. The plan for the climax of the celebration was for one of the goddesses to set off hundreds of rockets with her torch from atop the arch.[151] Unfortunately, a rogue rocket struck the arch, igniting the massive structure and the remaining rockets simultaneously and sending them into the air and down onto the expectant onlookers. A number of spectators were injured, including Peale himself. This event might have been the pinnacle of such Philadelphia festivities surrounding the events of the new nation, but it certainly wasn't the last. Upon arriving in Philadelphia on April 20, 1789, Washington was met with a great celebration at Gray's Ferry, on the Schuylkill River, several days into his seven-day procession from Mount Vernon to lower Manhattan, where he would be sworn in as the nation's first president. Greeted by a large crowd of spectators along with a discharge of artillery, the members of Washington's procession walked under twenty-foot high triumphal arches made of strands of laurels and cedar and past colorful flags representing the states and banners, decorated with a rattlesnake and a sun, respectively, which proclaimed "Don't Tread On Me" and "Behold The Rising Empire." Finally, the procession arrived at the highly decorated ferry that would take the group across the Schuylkill River. The crowd escorted Washington, along with state dignitaries and the leading citizens of the city, into Philadelphia.[152]

The same year Washington became president, Lewis entered into his second term in the Pennsylvania General Assembly and served as the first United States Attorney for the District of Pennsylvania, all while continuing to act as the primary counselor for the Pennsylvania Abolition Society and building his law practice. Luckily for Lewis, a man living in the busiest, most populated port city in the nation, who was coming into the most prolific time in his career, he had had the foresight to create an escape—a retreat for his family and a place to entertain his friends and business associates—a country villa he named Summerville. On July 4, 1789, Lewis and his wife Rosanna would host a dinner to celebrate United States independence, a newly inaugurated president, and the unveiling of their newly completed summer home.

The day after the party, Lewis's good friend William Rawle wrote in his journal that he "dined with Lewis at his villa—which one would not from the conversation have taken for Tusculum."[153] This description of Summerville would have suited Lewis, as it invoked the Roman City of Tusculum, whose beautiful rolling hills were brought to mind while looking out over the gorgeous view across the property and out toward the Schuylkill River. Rawle described the event as a "merry and sociable assemblage" of

*William Rawle's journal, July 4, 1789, noting "Dined with Lewis at his Villa….
" Journals of William Rawle, Sr., Rawle Family Papers, Historical Society of Pennsylvania.*

guests, including members of the Chew, Shippen, Tilghman, and Biddle families, among others. Rawle noted that during the dinner Lewis's "lawyer" demeanor was nowhere in sight and that the party would have continued long past two in the morning had it not been for some inclement weather.

Six years earlier, Lewis had purchased thirteen acres just a few miles from the city center. It wasn't far from "Fort Wilson," but it was worlds away from the heat and bustle of the city. With this land purchase Lewis proved that while still only in his early thirties, he was financially secure enough to become part of the coterie of wealthy Philadelphians who were following the trend of building summer retreats. Lewis didn't purchase just any piece of land but, rather, a prime location with beautiful and expansive views of the Schuylkill River. The property—which already had a long history with numerous owners before Lewis acquired it—contained a number of buildings, including a stone farmhouse believed to have been built by one of the previous owners.[154]

The stone house (noted in the property deed as a "messuage") would have been a starting point for Lewis. Whether he initially resided in the stone house is unknown. There is some indication that he may have rented the house and property to a local farmer for some time. Eventually though, Lewis decided to convert that simple farmhouse he had purchased into a grand mansion. One consideration that might have contributed to Lewis's decision to remake rather than build anew might have been the simple fact that the farmhouse was already perfectly situated to take advantage of the magnificent views overlooking the Schuylkill River. Lewis would have hired a known builder architect—perhaps even his brother-in-law John Lort, a member of the well regarded Carpenters' Company that had built Carpenters' Hall a few yards from Lewis's downtown home.[155] It is unknown when construction on Summerville actually started, but we are able to get a sense of timing through Lewis's correspondence. At the end of 1788 and into the early months of 1789, Lewis was engaged in settling an estate for a Mrs. Livingston, to whom he wrote:

> When I saw you this evening my dear Madam and appointed to see you at half past nine o'clock tomorrow morning I had really forgotten that I had appointed the same hour for meeting my Carpenters and Masons who are building for me on the banks of the Schuylkill. Will you therefore have the goodness to let me see you at any time between 2 & 3 o'clock tomorrow.[156]

Much of the original farmhouse remained structurally intact and become the core of the Lewis's new villa.[157] Similar to the remodeling done at nearby Mount Pleasant, the major change was to combine several smaller rooms to create a large central hallway and to extend the house so that the original entrance doorway became "central." Combined together, Lewis was able to create a design reflecting the federal style of architecture of the day, which had been popularized by the Adam brothers—Scotsmen who were greatly influenced by Roman architecture. The federal style was a move forward from the influences of the Georgian and Palladian styles that had been requisite in the early 1770s. The Adam brothers' Roman archeological explorations uncovered delicate decorative patterns of urns, swags, and garlands along with more flexible and free designs that revealed interior spaces of hexagonal, oval, and circular forms.[158] Like Lewis himself, his new home would be federalist, and would be set apart from the Middle-Georgian architecture of neighboring villas such as Mount Pleasant and Laurel Hill.

The interior of Summerville featured a grand center hall—a passageway with four statuary niches defined by reeded and carved woodwork and a plaster centerpiece on the ceiling. Each niche featured a statuary bust of white marble or black basalt. On either side of the passage were double doors with fanlights that opened into the reception rooms, whose mantels featured applied decorations in the federal style.[159] The federal style in America also ushered in the use of separate rooms for specific purposes and amenities like butlers' pantries and indoor privies. All of these details would enable Lewis to entertain in the grandest of style.

Strawberry Hill, watercolor by David J. Kennedy, 1870. David J. Kennedy Watercolors, Historical Society of Pennsylvania.

The exterior of the house remained rough stone but was likely stuccoed and scored to resemble ashlar blocks. This would have been especially helpful in covering up any joints between old and new construction as well as any differences in construction materials. Overall, the house has been described as "without ostentation . . . comfortable, commodious and quietly elegant."[160] In the end, Lewis would turn a simple farmhouse with a nice view into one of the most desirable and highly cultivated properties on the Schuylkill. Summerville would continue to serve as an important retreat for Lewis throughout his life.

It wasn't just Lewis and his friends who were enjoying the good life, however. Despite local political infighting and shaky financial stops and starts caused by the aftermath of the Revolution, the confidence of Philadelphia's citizens continued to grow along with the population. An act of Congress would make Philadelphia the nation's capitol in July of 1790. This and other factors allowed Philadelphians to enjoy ever more prosperous lives. Elegant and stylish houses were being built on every street. Those who weren't able to build a new home competed in a very tight rental market, outbidding one another to lease property. The middle class was now enjoying the luxuries previously enjoyed only by the upper class—fancy coaches and sedan chairs now filled the streets. Every man was looking forward and forgetting any past financial worries. As journalist Mathew Carey put it at the time, "extravagance was gradually eradicating the plain and wholesome habits of the city."[161]

In a few short years all of this exuberance would come to a screeching halt, and William Lewis would find himself at the epicenter of an unimaginable event in Philadelphia history—the 1793 yellow fever outbreak. Over the course of several months, Lewis would become both a patient and an advisor to Dr. Rush in the midst of great tragedy and a political firestorm.[162] Lewis would continue to stand by Rush as his good friend became a controversial figure in the arguments surrounding the causes and remedies of yellow fever, as he published his findings, and even as Rush left the Federalist party and started to associate himself with the Republicans. Later still, he would represent Rush in a high-profile libel case.

The once high-spirited Philadelphians found themselves in the middle of a hellish battle. While the first fatalities appeared in July of 1793, it would not be until August that the epidemic attracted attention from its citizens and officials, with the first official public notice from city officials published on August 22.[163] Victims initially experienced pains in the head, back, and limbs, accompanied by chills and a high fever. The fever would become more severe. Some said the eyes would be inflamed with a yellow color, others said the victim's skin turned a ghastly yellow shade. Eventually the victims would vomit black clots of blood caused by bleeding into the stomach. If not helped, death soon followed as the victim slipped into a helpless stupor. As stories started to circulate, the citizens finally started to take notice. Elizabeth Drinker recorded in her journal on August 23, 1793:

> A Fever prevails in the City, particularly in Water St. between Race and Arch Sts. of ye malignant kind; numbers have died of it. Some say it was occasioned by damaged Coffee and Fish, which were stored at Wm. Smiths'; others say it was imported in a Vessel from Cape Francois, which lay at our wharf, or at ye wharf back of our store. Doctor Hutchinson is ordered by ye Governor to enquire into ye report. He found, as 'tis said, upwards of 70 persons sick in that square of different disorders; several of this putrid or bilious fever. Some are ill in Water St. between Arch and Market Sts., and some in Race Street. 'Tis really an alarming and serious time.[164]

The College of Physicians, led by Dr. Rush, held a meeting to discuss the outbreak. At this point, the medical community was unaware of the link between the mosquito and the disease's progress. Most people at the time believed that yellow fever was a disease originating in rotting vegetable matter and putrefying filth; they also believed it to be contagious. Of the several recommendations made by the College of Physicians, the first and foremost was simply to leave the city. A good portion of the population did just that, along with members of Congress and President Washington and his cabinet. Congress and other officials set up in Germantown, just outside of the city, for the rest of the summer session. Eventually they all just headed home, with Washington returning to Mount Vernon. It has been estimated that during the months of August and September, seventeen thousand to upwards of twenty thousand persons left the city—almost half the population.

Edward Burd, who resided on Fourth Street not far from William Lewis, recorded, "My house is entirely Shut up—People dying all around it and no venturing there without risque, the Disorder being so easily taken that many people hardly know how they have caught ye Infection. From ye best Accounts I can collect there must have been 500 or 600 people buried last Week."[165]

We do not know exactly when Lewis or his family left the city or whether they went to Summerville or to stay with relatives in Chester County. We do know that Lewis was witness to much of what Mathew Carey described as the constant activity of carts, wagons, and coaches transporting family and furniture in all directions as the citizens closed up their homes, leaving nothing behind except a servant or two to guard their abodes. He would have seen house after house in his neighborhood left abandoned, the empty streets, and the "death carts" transporting bodies running consistently past his home. He would have looked out his window and seen the suffering awaiting Dr. Rush or seeking counsel from Bishop White, just across Chestnut Street. Those who remained in the city utilized any number of recommended remedies: using vinegar and camphor as a disinfectant, burning fires in the middle of the streets, smoking tobacco and cigars, and chewing garlic or stuffing cloves into their shoes and pockets.[166] Obviously, Lewis—an incessant smoker—was not helped by the presence of "purifying" smoke. We know nothing of his battle with the fever other than that Dr. Rush listed Lewis as his first yellow fever patient when he published his findings. As such, Lewis would have likely received Rush's "heroic medicine," an aggressive approach that included copious bleeding and ingesting large quantities of mercury. We might also speculate that Lewis recovered from his bout of fever before he left for the country. We do know that he eventually took his leave, confessing to Rush in a letter, "I never left Philadelphia with so much pleasure as yesterday nor never found Such Pleasure in the Country as I do today."[167]

As days passed, the public offices, the city library, the coffee houses, and even the churches began to close their doors. Even the newspapers—in the midst of their heated debate over the causes and treatments of the fever—decided to close up shop. The deaths increased as many victims were left to their own devices with no support at all—the poorest of the city being the hardest hit. Yellow fever victims started dying so quickly that there were hardly enough people left to bury them. Large pits were dug in locations such as the potters' field across from the Walnut Street debtor's prison (now Washington Square Park) to allow for mass burials of ten, fifteen, or more bodies at one time. By October 2, a newspaper in New York remarked that in Philadelphia, "the only business was grave-digging."[168]

Stephen Girard's new Bush Hill Hospital, run by Dr. Jean Devèze, offered an alternative to Rush's aggressive treatments. The Bush Hill contingent did not believe that yellow fever was contagious; they took in anyone who needed help and offered gentle treatments of quiet rest and cool compresses. By mid-October the worst of the fever had passed. Dr. Rush's theories and treatments were challenged by his colleagues, leading to a falling-out with the College of Physicians and, ultimately, to his dismissal. Despite this fact, Rush hoped to publish his ideas and sought the advice of his closest friends. Samuel Meredith—also a patient, who was said to have been over-bled under Rush's care—urged him not to publish. Tench Coxe advised him to delay publication at least until Congress had reconvened. Bishop White and Lewis urged him to move forward.

Rush went ahead and published his observations and opinions in *An Account of the Bilious remitting Yellow Fever, as it Appeared in the City of Philadelphia, in the Year 1793*. In the preface, dated June 14, 1794, he wrote that his hope was to publish the information as soon as possible in case the disease should reappear in the current season. He also admitted that the book had "been hastily copied from my notes." Later in 1799, he would publish a longer, more thorough version, *Observations Upon the Origin of the Malignant Bilious, or Yellow Fever in Philadelphia, and Upon the Means of Preventing It: Addressed to the Citizens of Philadelphia*. By publishing a list of his initial yellow fever patients, such as William Lewis, Rush indicated in his report that he hoped his remedy would assure his fellow citizens that the disease was no longer incurable.[169] While Lewis was a lucky survivor, the overall survival rate of Dr. Rush's patients was not known to be great. While Dr. Rush's intentions were genuine, it turns out that the doctors at Bush Hill were more successful in helping their patients recover. In the end, yellow fever would claim well over four thousand citizens of the city.

With the cool air of the fall season finally arriving, Philadelphia eventually returned to some degree of normalcy. Despite the depths of tragedy from which they had come, the citizens of Philadelphia bounced back fairly quickly. Families returned to their homes, and those who were able reopened their businesses. The president returned to the city on November 30, and Congress had enough members to convene on December 2. It would not take long before Philadelphia once again became the center of heated debate and turmoil.

Dr. Rush had hoped that his publication would help to advance the field of medicine by encouraging discussion among his colleagues. Instead, he was severely attacked by the press, especially in the local newspapers. William Cobbett, a British citizen who wrote under the pseudonym Peter Porcupine, kept up sustained assaults on Rush's remedies of purging and bleeding. Cobbett believed that testimonies extolling the virtues of Rush's remedies had been falsely published. Finally, in October 1797, Rush sued Cobbett for libel, declaring that he was politically motivated and calling him out for his pro-British rhetoric.[170] The case was tried in the Supreme Court of Pennsylvania, with Rush represented by the formidable team of William Lewis, John Hopkinson, Moses Levy, and Jared Ingersoll. Cobbett was represented by William Rawle, Robert G. Harper, and Edward Tilghman. It was reported in the local paper that the pleadings on both sides were lengthy, ingenious, and eloquent.[171] The case hinged upon the doctrine of libels and the liberty of the press. The verdict of the jury was in favor of Rush. In the hopes that this case would be exemplary, the damages in the case were liberal. Although the court awarded Rush five thousand dollars, Cobbett quickly escaped back to Britain to avoid making restitution.

Beyond the tragedy of the yellow fever epidemic, Philadelphians continued to focus on the French Revolution, especially as the city continued to become home to an ever-expanding population of French refugees. France declared war on Great Britain and the Netherlands. This trouble between France and England would further complicate the foreign policy decisions being debated by the Washington administration—and would do so for many years to come. Lewis understood that the delicate balance between the United States and France, the United States and Britain, and Britain and France would require extreme caution and calculation. This was not an occasion for celebration or a time to take sides. While Lewis would have been annoyed by the young women in bright, tricolor costumes parading to music around the French minister's home at Market and Twelfth Streets, he would have been completely repulsed by the demonstration of a French guillotine—complete with rolling head—at Market and Tenth Streets.

Beyond the political intrigue, Philadelphia offered its residents and visitors many other frivolous diversions. Ricketts's Circus had returned to the city, offering equestrian displays, tumblers, performing dogs, and clowns. And thanks to a diligent crowd of drama enthusiasts, the New Theater (Chestnut Street Theater) was finally allowed to reopen after a bill passed through Pennsylvania's General Assembly. Located a block south of the President's House and just across from the State House, its premiere production was "School for Scandal," which was said to be Washington's favorite. The theater offered a wide array of entertainments—from Shakespeare to a French tightrope walker called Monsieur Placide, and even a one-night stand of "Leap through a Barrel of Fire"—to pique the interest of the varied crowd who purchased tickets.[172] Ever the showman, Charles Willson Peale moved his "Repository for

Natural Curiosities" to Philosophical Hall in the State House yard. He used his artistic skills to paint backgrounds and taught himself taxidermy to arrange specimens of creatures for public display. Dr. Morgan's collection of assembled mastodon bones was also included in the museum, as was Peale's portrait gallery, which featured all the patriotic leaders.[173]

As Charles Willson Peale expanded his portrait gallery, the artist Gilbert Stuart arrived in town in November of 1794 with the purpose of painting a portrait of President Washington. While Peale focused on portraits of the "patriots," Stuart turned his eye to Philadelphia's social elite during the time that the city served as the nation's capitol. Stuart's uncle was the merchant Joseph Anthony, who had ties to William Bingham, John Vaughan, and Thomas Willing. Most importantly, Stuart had an introductory letter from John Jay—the successful negotiator of the British Treaty—which served as another useful entry to the Federalist contingent in Philadelphia. Key to his access to President Washington would be his acquaintance with William Bingham and his wife, Anne Willing Bingham, whom he had met previously in London.[174] During his time in Philadelphia, Stuart would paint portraits of both William and Anne as well as all of Anne's sisters (the daughters of Thomas Willing). President Washington would sit for the first of several Stuart portraits starting in 1795. Many of Stuart's sitters had close connections to the president and his wife, Martha. William Lewis sat for a portrait sometime in 1797 or 1798. Additionally, Lewis purchased one of Stuart's portraits of Washington. Both paintings were hung at Summerville.[175]

William Dunlap commented that Stuart's work "left us the features of those who have achieved immortality for themselves, and made known others who would but for his art have slept in the merited obscurity." Indeed, Stuart's portraits have provided insight into the lives of those who lived alongside the patriot heroes, especially the women, who wouldn't otherwise have been recognized. Stuart's paintings would also become an important ingredient in the foundation of another seminal Philadelphia institution, the Pennsylvania Academy of Fine Arts.

Inspired by merchants who had formed the New York Academy of the Fine Arts, a similar group in Philadelphia came together to form their own academy—the Pennsylvania Academy of Fine Arts. Unlike earlier attempts made by Charles Willson Peale and his fellow artists to create such an academy, the principal organizers of PAFA came from the legal and business community. On December 26, 1805, members met at Independence Hall to sign an application for an act of incorporation. Of the seventy individuals who signed the petition, forty-one were Philadelphia lawyers, including William Lewis. Only three signers were actually artists, Charles Willson Peale, his son Rembrandt Peale, and the sculptor William Rush.[176] What was important, however, was the fact that many of Philadelphia's leading families quickly realized the importance of not just supporting the academy but bequeathing their treasured portraits to its collections. [177]

In addition to the Academy of Fine Arts, William Lewis would help establish the first law library in the United States. In 1802, seventy-one members of the Philadelphia bar were incorporated as the Law Library Company of the City of Philadelphia. With its mission to keep a common professional library and to professionally educate young men, the library accumulated close to four hundred volumes of texts, commentaries, and decisions deemed useful for this purpose. At the time, very little was written or available for American lawyers, so the items collected were chiefly written by British authors. The first officers of the association were all the prominent members of the bar, including William Lewis, Joseph

McKean, Edward Tilghman, and William Rawle. The Law Library of Philadelphia would eventually become the Philadelphia Bar Association, which is considered the oldest continuous bar association in the United States.[178]

Just as important to Lewis as establishing the Law Library was his role as mentor, educator, and friend to a number of aspiring young lawyers in Philadelphia. In contrast to his own relatively humble background upon arrival in the office of Nicholas Waln, many of Lewis's students were sons of prominent Philadelphia families who recognized that the success Lewis had attained at the bar offered their children an outstanding educational opportunity. Although we know of no official student register, many of these men achieved such prominence, whether in law or in another field, that their association with Lewis was recorded. Among those trained by Lewis were future statesmen and attorneys such as Peter Du Ponceau, Isaac Wayne, Samuel Roberts, Richard Rush, Nicholas Biddle, and Major William Jackson.

Peter Stephen Du Ponceau, a young Frenchman, was among Lewis's earliest students. Born in June of 1760 in Saint-Martin-de-Ré, Du Ponceau came to America in 1777 as the secretary and English translator for Baron von Steuben whose role was to help organize the American military. In 1781 an illness forced him to leave the military, but he remained in Philadelphia. He began to work as undersecretary for Secretary of Foreign Affairs Robert Livingston—a position which offered valuable training in international law. When Livingston left the position, Du Ponceau decided to study law and, at the age of thirty-two, entered into Lewis's office to pursue his studies. Livingston, upon hearing of Du Ponceau's new arrangement, wrote him to say, "I rejoice most sincerely in your happy establishment which I cannot but hope will be the harbinger of more important appointments hereafter." Du Ponceau recalled Lewis as an "able master" who "had always been ready to assist me with his lessons and his advice." While studying law, Du Ponceau worked as an interpreter for the Pennsylvania Supreme Executive Council. He was admitted to the bar in June of 1785. By the fall of that year, he had twenty-one cases on the docket for the Court of Common Pleas for the City and County of Philadelphia.[179]

Du Ponceau would earn his place among the most prominent Philadelphia lawyers and would help found the Philadelphia Law Association in 1802 and the Law Academy of Philadelphia in 1821. He was a member of the American Philosophical Society and the Athenaeum Society, a director of the Library Company, and a founder and president of the Historical Society of Pennsylvania. He was also a founding member of the French Benevolent Society of Philadelphia. He is heralded today for his linguistic achievements in Native American and Chinese languages. At his death in 1844 at the age of eighty-four, he was the oldest member of the Philadelphia Bar.

Upon the recommendation of a mutual friend, the famous Revolutionary War General Anthony Wayne looked no further than Lewis when seeking professional training for his only son, Isaac. Born near Paoli, Pennsylvania, in 1768, Isaac graduated from Dickinson College in 1792. After studying law with Lewis, he was admitted to both the Chester County and Philadelphia bars in 1795. In 1799 he was elected to the United States House of Representatives and later would serve in the Pennsylvania State Senate. He would follow in his father's military footsteps by becoming a captain in the cavalry during the War of 1812. He was later promoted to colonel in the Pennsylvania Volunteer Infantry. Wayne returned to politics after the war, but eventually retired to his farm in Waynesborough (Paoli), where he farmed for the remainder of his life. He died in 1852 and is buried at the St. David's Episcopal Church (in present-day Wayne, Pennsylvania, formerly referred to as Radnor).

Samuel Roberts, who was born in Philadelphia in September of 1761, likely began his apprenticeship with Lewis in 1790. He was admitted to the bar in 1793. Pennsylvania Governor Thomas McKean appointed Roberts a judgeship in the Fifth Circuit in April of 1803—a circuit that would eventually encompass Allegheny, Washington, Beaver, Fayette, Greene, Westmoreland and Butler Counties. The greatly respected Judge Roberts remained on the bench until his death on December 13, 1820.[180] One obituary praised him for having "established a character for soundness of opinions, and just judicial decision, which gave him an exalted station in the judiciary of Pennsylvania."[181]

It comes as no surprise that Richard Rush, the third of thirteen children born to Dr. Benjamin Rush and his wife, Julia Stockton Rush, would become Lewis's student. Dr. Rush and Lewis were neighbors, friends, and collaborators. Richard, born in August of 1780, entered Princeton College (then called the College of New Jersey) at age fourteen; three years later, in 1797, he graduated as the youngest member of his class. He studied law with William Lewis until the age of twenty, when he was admitted to the bar in the year 1800. He became a highly successful trial lawyer before serving in government; he was appointed Pennsylvania Attorney General in 1811. Having attracted the attention of President Madison, Richard Rush was named comptroller of the U.S. Treasury in 1812. From 1814 to 1817 he served as Attorney-General of the United States, and in 1817, he was appointed acting secretary of state under President James Monroe. He was then appointed minister to the Court of St. James, a post he held from 1817 through 1825. As a result of his efforts, he is now widely credited by historians for restoring diplomatic ties with Great Britain after the War of 1812. From 1825 to 1829 Rush served under John Quincy Adams as secretary of the United States Treasury. In 1836, he was again sent to Great Britain, to secure the estate of John Smithson on behalf of the United States. This bequest was later used to found the Smithsonian Institution in Washington, D.C. In 1847 Rush was again asked to return to Europe, this time as minister to France under President Polk, a post he held until 1851. After a long and distinguished career as a public servant, Richard Rush died on July 13, 1859, and was buried in the family vault in North Laurel Hill Cemetery in Philadelphia.[182]

Perhaps Lewis's most recognizable student was Nicholas Biddle. Biddle was a descendant of an English family who had arrived in Philadelphia with William Penn. Born in Philadelphia in January of 1786, he was the fourth son of Charles Biddle, a prominent merchant and politician. He was extraordinarily bright and entered the University of Pennsylvania at a young age. He later transferred to Princeton—which offered a liberal arts–based curriculum—where at the age of fifteen he graduated as class valedictorian.

Upon graduating Princeton, Biddle proceeded to study law with William Lewis. Soon after, however, he accepted the position of Secretary to the United States Minister to France in 1804. Lewis was one of Biddle's strongest supporters and had recommended him for the position. In response to Biddle's promise that he would eagerly learn his new position, Lewis wrote, "should you ever think of me I beg of you to remember that I shall by no means be satisfied with hearing that you are in good health and conduct yourself with propriety. I shall expect much more, I shall, whenever I hear your name mentioned expect to hear that you are in the pursuit of noble ends by noble means and that your success and your merit bid fair to render your character eminently prominent among the sons of America."[183]

Shortly thereafter Biddle was summoned to England as secretary to James Monroe, the United

States Minister to the Court of St. James. In 1807, he returned to Philadelphia and practiced law, only to decide law was not his passion. In 1810, Biddle was elected to the Pennsylvania House of Representatives, where he proposed the concept of public schools that became the basis for Pennsylvania's school system today. Biddle became interested in banking and finance and in 1819 was appointed by President James Monroe to become a government director of the Second Bank of the United States. He would become the bank's president in 1823, at age thirty-seven. He is also credited in establishing Girard College under Stephen Girard's will. Biddle died in February, 1844, at his Philadelphia estate, Andalusia, at age fifty-eight. He was remembered as "a scholar, a man of business, and "a man who "had the requisites of a statesman."[184]

Perhaps not as well known as Nicholas Biddle, but certainly equally respected, was Lewis's student Major William Jackson. Born in England in 1759 and an orphan by age sixteen, William Jackson was sent to South Carolina under the guardianship of Colonel Owen Roberts. There he was commissioned as an officer in the First Regiment of the South Carolina Infantry. As part of the growing Continental Army, Jackson participated in the southern campaigns and was eventually promoted to captain-major in October of 1779. As secretary to Colonel John Laurens, Jackson participated in several diplomatic missions in Europe. Despite his attachment to the military, Jackson eventually settled down in Philadelphia and studied law with William Lewis. Jackson was admitted to the Court of Common Pleas in June of 1788 and shortly thereafter to the bar of the Supreme Court of Pennsylvania. He became secretary to the Constitutional Convention in Philadelphia in 1787 and also secretary in the exclusive Order of the Cincinnati. During this time he became close to President Washington and was made his personal secretary in 1788. Jackson served the president until 1791, when he resigned. Several years later, in 1796, Jackson was appointed by Washington to surveyor of customs for the Port of Philadelphia, where he served until 1801. Jackson died on December 17, 1828, and was buried at Christ Church in Philadelphia.

Many people don't realize that they have often seen an image of Major Jackson—as the man in the bright red coat with a highly prominent position—in Howard Chandler Christy's much-loved 1940 painting depicting the signing of the United States Constitution at Independence Hall. The painting is most often used as an illustration in history books, but it actually hangs in the east stairway in the House side of the United States Capitol. Major Jackson appears in the center of the portrait, just behind the seated Ben Franklin, with his arm raised in apparent acknowledgement of those who wish to sign the document.

Of all of Lewis's students, Major Jackson would become one of his closest friends and advocates. In the end, Jackson would be the one to pen the published Lewis obituary. Jackson's relationship with President Washington would play a significant part in Lewis agreeing to become Judge of the District Court of Pennsylvania. While working as Washington's secretary, Jackson would actually spend some time living in the Washington household. His proximity to Washington brought him well into the inner circle of Philadelphia's social elite where he would meet his wife, Elizabeth Willing—daughter of Thomas Willing and niece of Elizabeth Willing Powel. Her sister Ann married William Bingham, one of the richest men in the country and her sister Abigail would marry Judge Richard Peters. Abigail Adams, wife of John Adams, had declared the five Willing sisters—Mary, Anne, Elizabeth, Dorothy, and Abigail—a "constellation of beauties" during a visit to Philadelphia.

Just over the garden fence from the constellation of beauties—as the Lewis family garden at Fort Wilson backed up to that of the Willing household—were Lewis's own daughters. From the few accounts we have of Margaret and Martha Lewis, they seem to have been strong-minded women. At the age of nineteen, oldest daughter Margaret appears to have eloped in August of 1792 at Old Swede's Church in Philadelphia, for her marriage record reads: "Stephen Agard and Margaret Lewis. He from Barbadoes—she from Bucks County, daughter of John and Elizabeth Lewis. This woman was daughter of a respectable father in Phila but assumed false parental names."[185]

The question of why Margaret felt the need to assume false parental names is unknown. Her mother, Rosanna Lort, a direct descendent of the founders of Old Swedes, would have been well known to the church administrators. It is likely they did not have the consent of her parents to marry, but we have no knowledge of what Lewis and his wife might have found wanting in Stephen Agard as a son-in-law. Agard was the son of an English planter in Barbados and "came to Philadelphia engaged in the wholesale and retail grocery business." He was also on record as a student at what is now the University of Pennsylvania for the year 1791.[186] Three years later Margaret would give birth to a daughter, Martha, who would die in infancy. She would eventually give birth to two more daughters: another Martha, born in 1798, and Louisa.

Martha, Lewis's youngest daughter, married Dr. Samuel F. Conover in 1795. She died a short four years later, on February 17, 1799, at the age of twenty-five, not long after the birth of her son, Lewis H. Conover. *Claypoole's Daily Advertiser* ran the following obituary:

> On the 17th of Feb, departed this life, Mrs. Martha Conover, of this city, wife of Dr. Conover, and daughter of William Lewis, Esq. Of this amiable lady it may with truth be said that she was an instructive companion, a kind and benevolent neighbor, and affectionate wife, and an endearing mother. During a tedious and severe illness, she displayed uncommon fortitude, and when the awful summons arrived, evinced an equal degree of resignation.[187]

A month later, on March 28, 1799, Lewis's son, Josiah, would marry Margaret Delany.[188] The ceremony was conducted by their neighbor Bishop White at Christ Church. The bride's father, Sharp Delany, worked as a federal customs collector and is credited with helping Alexander Hamilton develop the Revenue Cutter Bill, which allowed for the building of special ships to help enforce customs laws. Margaret would give birth to their first child, a daughter named Margaret Delany Lewis, in January 1800.

Amid the marriages, the death of Martha Lewis, and the birth of several grandchildren came another family tragedy. In September of 1800, Lewis's wife Rosanna died at the age of forty-nine. For twenty-nine years Rosanna had been by Lewis's side through all his struggles and triumphs. No one would have blamed Lewis if he had felt a bit like Martha Washington, who had written after the death of her beloved, "I shall soon follow . . . I have no more trials to pass." It doesn't appear, however, that Lewis related to Martha's state of mind, as he had a lot more life left in him—and just as much fight.

As it turned out, Lewis's daughter Margaret Agard would soon lose her spouse as well. Quite ironically for the daughter of the man who made an international name pursuing justice in dealing with French privateering, her husband's fate ended up in the hands of pirates. After the death of his father,

Stephen Agard traveled to Barbados to settle the estate. Upon his return, he set sail for Philadelphia with a large cargo of merchandise, but the ship was captured. It was reported that the pirates murdered all aboard except for Agard and the captain who were taken to a foreign port, locked in a dungeon, and released only after their captors sailed away. With weak health and a broken spirit, Agard managed to return to his mother's home in Barbados, only to die there a few weeks later.[189] Poor Margaret had lost her sister, her mother, and her husband in quick succession and was left alone with her two young daughters. William Lewis would step in to ensure not just the wellbeing of his daughter but the future of his granddaughters as well.

Lewis does not appear to be a man interested in wallowing in tragedy. Within six months of his wife's death, he was ready to marry a second time. On January 23, 1801, Lewis married Frances Esmond Durdin. Like his son, Josiah, Lewis chose to be married at Christ Church by his friend Bishop White.[190] Frances, herself a widow for a number of years, was born in Ireland to Sir Thomas Esmond, Baronet. She married her first husband, Richard Durdin, before immigrating to America. Frances and Richard had three children, Richard Jr., Frances Maria Esmond, and Alexander.[191] The Durdins built an estate in Bucks County on the Delaware River, about twenty-seven miles north of Philadelphia. At the time of her husband's death, the property, known as Richland, consisted of more than five thousand acres, including a house, a granary, a coach-house, a barn, stables, tenant houses, three orchards, a shad fishery, and a boat landing. Richland was put up for sale according to Richard Durdin's estate directive. A sales advertisement in Dunlap's *American Daily Advertiser* boasted: "Any person inclining to purchase, can only be convinced of its value, by taking a view of it." Frances, however, would keep another property in Sunbury, Northumberland County (Pennsylvania), on the eastern bank of the Susquehanna River. There is some further indication that she owned and spent some time at an additional property in Luzerne County. Frances' papers include letters she received from her husband (then William Lewis) addressed to her at "near Beach Grove, Luzerne County." [192]

Correspondence shows that William and Fanny (as Lewis called his wife) enjoyed a loving relationship. On November 24, 1803, Lewis presented Frances with a Bible bearing an inscription written in Lewis's hand: "This Bible is the property of: 'Frances Lewis; presented to her by her affectionate Husband, W. Lewis.'" Correspondence also shows that they were involved in the lives of each others' children. Frances's oldest son, Richard, would die in July of 1809 in Philadelphia, and her daughter, Frances Maria, would die several years later in December of 1812, also in Philadelphia. At some point, records show that Frances adopted a child called Maria Ada (later Fisher). She was born on March 14, 1810, and is sometimes referred to as a granddaughter. It is possible that she was the daughter of Frances Maria, but no records have proven this as yet. Frances's youngest child, Alexander, was a troubled soul. He would leave Philadelphia and move to St. Croix, where

William Lewis, Esq., without his wig (artist unknown). Society Portrait Collection, Historical Society of Pennsylvania.

Miniature of Francis Durdin (artist and date unknown). Photo from the author's collection.

he also would also die before his mother in April of 1821. It would be Maria Ada who would remain close to Frances throughout her life.

By 1817, son Josiah and daughter-in-law Margaret added eight more children to their family, including their first son, honored with the name William Lewis, who was born in March 1801. Their second son, Josiah Jr., born in 1811, would die at the age of four. Most of the rest of their children would outlive the parents, including two more born in later years. Of course, both Frances and Lewis continued to look after Lewis's widowed daughter, Margaret, and her children, Martha and Louisa Agard. In an 1810 letter written to his Josiah, Lewis informed him, "I have placed Peggy and her children in a small neat house on Bachan Hill [sic] where she has a good garden, orchard and pasture of about 4 acres."[193]

Even with her father's support, Margaret and her daughters appeared to live their lives of their own accord. This was apparent on the occasion when the two girls accompanied their mother to Edgmont for a family visit to the home of Lewis's brother. While there, the girls met and fell in love with their future husbands.[194] Martha's beau was George Green, Jr., and Louisa's was his cousin Samuel Green. When George and Martha decided to marry they found both of their families opposed it. George's father, George Green, Sr., a prosperous farmer, had already selected the daughter of his neighbor Joseph Bishop for his son's wife. He thought Martha Agard—a city girl—ill suited to be a farmer's wife. He forbade his son to marry Martha, even threatening to cut his son off if he went through with it. Lewis had similar concerns about the marriage. He wanted more for his granddaughter. The result of all this opposition was that the couple eloped, just as Martha's mother had done more than twenty years before.[195]

Six

Profound Lawyer:

Lewis Establishes Precedents for a New Nation

America's burgeoning foreign policy stance, the need to protect trade and commerce, and the effects of federal decisions on domestic affairs would continue to create even greater opportunities for William Lewis. His particular knowledge in commerce, especially as it pertained to trade and maritime law, made him an expert sought out as counsel in what would be considered the highest-profile cases of the time. From mid-1790 to the early 1800s Lewis was involved in more than fifty cases dealing with commercial law alone. He would dominate the field and become "nationally known for his unsurpassed knowledge of commercial law."[196] His cases involved issues of slavery, British debt, privateering, and treason, among others. Regardless of the particular issue, Lewis always worked to insure the rights of the individual while maintaining the intent of the law—always challenging the courts on their interpretation regardless of whether they chose to follow his lead. Further, the intensity and seriousness with which Lewis approached each case—whether a small real estate transaction or a

"W. Lewis," engraving by C. Goodman and R. Piggot. Simon Gratz Collection, Historical Society of Pennsylvania.

65

hotly debated, high-profile affair—helped set the tone for the future of the United States court system, from local jurisdictions through to the United States Supreme Court. Professor G. S. Rowe, discussing the Pennsylvania Supreme Court in *The Embattled Bench*, notes, "perhaps more than any other figure, the lawyer William Lewis offered the judges a variety of creative legal arguments by which to advance social, economic, and legal reforms."[197] Today we trust that, on the whole, United States citizens will receive a fair trial and that our courts are not subject to the vagaries of whichever politicians are in power. Likewise, we view the Supreme Court of the United States as the ultimate interpreter of our Constitution. At the close of the eighteenth century, the court systems of our newly formed government had not yet earned such a reputation. It was the dedication of lawyers such as William Lewis who would set such high standards during this time period.

A selection of Lewis's caseload:

Respublica v. Keppele, Pennsylvania Supreme Court, 1793:

The case of *Respublica v. Keppele* involved an eleven-year-old boy named Benjamin Harris, who was bound by indenture as a servant to Catharine Keppele until his fifteenth birthday by consent of Harris's guardian when the boy was just an infant.[198] When Harris ran away at the age of fourteen, his master ordered him jailed. Lewis petitioned the court to free the boy from his servitude by a writ of habeas corpus. Lewis's arguments centered on his belief that indentured servitude was extremely degrading:

> If they run away, they shall serve five days for one. If they deal with other persons, they shall make satisfaction by servitude, to double the value of the goods. If they marry, they incur an additional servitude of one whole year after their time by indenture is expired. If they set fire to the woods, they shall be whipped with twenty-one lashes, &c. The difference then between them and apprentices is sufficiently obvious.[199]

Lewis's argument won out. The Supreme Court voided the indenture, agreeing that a "guardian cannot have the power of putting his ward in the degrading situation of a servant, and therefore the lad must be dismissed."[200] This ruling helped to set the precedent that servitude of native-born minors and American-born adults would no longer be tolerated. The court took additional steps to protect immigrant indentured servants by holding their masters to the most rigorous of procedural standards. The actions of the court showed that indentured servitude as an institution was deemed at odds with the new republican realities.[201]

Georgia v. Brailsford, United States Supreme Court, 1794:

When the United States Supreme Court opened their session February 3, 1794, first on the docket was *Georgia v. Brailsford*, a case that had been postponed in August of the previous year when the court was forced to flee Philadelphia during the yellow fever outbreak. This case attracted much public attention, perhaps because it had begun in the United States District Court of Georgia in the fall of 1791 as a simple suit between individuals over recovery of debt and had turned into a much more difficult matter that eventually became the first jury trial to be held in the Supreme Court of the United States.[202] The preeminent lawyers of the time represented the parties: Alexander Dallas and

Jared Ingersoll for the state of Georgia and William Bradford, the current acting U.S. attorney general, Edward Tilghman, and William Lewis for the defendants.

The original case was instituted by Samuel Brailsford—for himself as well as fellow merchants Robert William Powell and John Hopton—against James Spalding, who with his partners Roger Kelsall and Job Colcock owed the Brailsford group more than seven thousand pounds British sterling on a bond dated September 21, 1774. As early as November 1790 an attorney representing Brailsford & Co. petitioned the federal circuit court in Georgia to issue process against Spalding, but the suit was discontinued. The suit was reinstituted during the following term of the court in April 1791, but this time Brailsford's attorney used the words "aliens" and "subjects of his Brittannick Majesty" when referring to his clients—a notion that would become a critical factor in that it caused the defendant Spalding to put forth a plea that did not deny that the debt existed. Instead, he maintained he was under no obligation to pay the plaintiffs because the state of Georgia had a right to recover them under statutes passed by the legislature before the Treaty of Peace with Great Britain had been signed.[203] The state of Georgia then stepped in to ask admittance to the case so that the state's interests could be directly represented and that both money claims—the state's and the British creditors'—could be settled in a single lawsuit. Spalding's counsel, however, would not allow it, and the court had no precedent that would have allowed them to bypass the wishes of the defense. The case went forward without including the considerations of the state of Georgia. The Georgia circuit court judges ruled unanimously against Spalding. The state of Georgia, fearful that Brailsford might be repaid his debt before their claim to it could be heard, moved to file a "bill in equity" against Brailsford and his partners and Spalding. The bill—filed in the United States Supreme Court on August 8, 1792 by Alexander Dallas—asked for an injunction on any funds collected by Brailsford or future payments made by Spalding, as they believed that the treaty had transferred the debt from Brailsford and vested it in the state and that the state of Georgia had never relinquished claim to said debt.

Although a split decision, the U.S. Supreme Court justices in the majority thought that granting an injunction provided the only viable procedure for giving the court more time to decide how to get all the parties with claims to the debt before the court. They agreed that the money "should remain in the custody of the law, till the law has adjudged to whom it belongs."[204] After much discussion, a plan was enacted to allow for a common law action between Georgia and Brailsford—a novel endeavor.

When the U.S. Supreme Court resumed in February 1794, a special jury was summoned. The question at hand was to whom Spalding should pay his debt—to Brailsford or the state of Georgia? In the end it was determined that while Georgia law may have prevented defendants' rights to recover sequestered funds during the war with Britain, the peace treaty allowed that the "real owner of the debt" was the same after the war as during the war—Brailsford, not Georgia. The jury ruled in favor of the defendant. Georgia's "bill in equity" was dismissed and dissolved on February 14, 1794. This case had allowed the U.S. Supreme Court to grapple with the limits of its equitable and common law jurisdictions, to make its first pronouncements on treaties as the supreme law of the land, and to establish precedents for dealing with similar questions in the future. [205]

John Nicholson, Pennsylvania State Senate, March 1794:

John Nicholson had been working as the first comptroller general for the state of Pennsylvania (appointed in April 1782), where he managed state financial affairs, including collecting and receiving taxes and liquidating the estates of those found guilty of treason. In April of 1793, the State House of Representatives impeached Nicholson for allegedly diverting funds when he had exchanged state "new loan" certificates for federal securities.[206] A committee was also appointed to examine Nicholson's accounts. The committee reported Nicholson a defaulter, which caused the Pennsylvania State Senate to bring suit against Nicholson for recovery of the alleged diverted funds. William Lewis led the charge for Nicholson's defense. One wonders if Lewis was politically motivated to take on this case, for Albert Gallatin had been one of the state senators leading the charge against Nicholson, and it was at this time that Lewis was leading the charge to keep Gallatin from keeping his new position in the United States Senate. The Nicholson trial would proceed on February 26, 1794.

Jacob Hiltzheimer provided brief insights on the trial in his diary:

> March 4 [1794].—The trial of John Nicholson was resumed and Mr. Morgan [chairman of the committee appointed by the House to investigate] concluded his presentation of the charges against him.
>
> . . . .
>
> March 19.—William Lewis, Esq., spoke two hours on behalf of Nicholson.
>
> . . . .
>
> April 11.—Was informed that John Nicholson resigned his office of Comptroller General after the Senate had decided in his favor, and that John Donaldson was appointed in his place.[207]

Lewis and his co-counselors were successful in their defense despite the fact that the case became prolonged and confusing. In the end, the house prosecutors were never able to gain the two-thirds majority vote needed to uphold the charge. In fact, several house members voted in favor of Nicholson.

Nicholson went on to create the North American Land Company a year later with his partner Robert Morris. The two speculated heavily, purchasing and promoting land and business deals in Washington, D.C., Pennsylvania, Virginia, North Carolina, South Carolina, Georgia, and Kentucky. Their schemes proved unprofitable, and both men ended up in debtors' prison. Nicholson died in prison in late 1800, leaving his wife and eight children more than four million dollars in debt. His estate papers were sequestered by a state commission, and an attempt was made to settle his debts, a process that would continue for more than forty years.[208]

Ware, Administrator of Jones v. Hylton, et al., United States Supreme Court, 1796:

Lewis's most famous case, and perhaps his most influential in setting precedent, is *Ware, Administrator of Jones v. Hylton, et al.*[209] Justice James Iredell characterized the case as "the greatest Cause which ever came before a Judicial Court *in the World*." The outcome of the case would decide the fate of any number of American debtors and their British creditors.[210] According to Maeva Marcus, editor of the *Documentary History of the Supreme Court*, when the federal courts opened in 1790, British creditors leaped at the opportunity to finally sue their debtors. The largest burden of this debt was held by the people of Virginia. The state had decided not to deal with the British in their own courts; additionally, they believed the British had carried off their slaves at the end of the Revolutionary War.

Important points arising from the arguments and decisions in the case touched on the definition and nature of war, the sovereign status of American states, the power and usage of international enemy confiscation laws, the preeminence of the federal constitution over state statutes, the operation of eminent domain, the status of private debts owed to enemies during war, and the operation of a peace treaty upon such debts and upon state statute.

Ware v. Hylton arose from an act passed by the commonwealth of Virginia in 1777, during the Revolutionary War, that allowed the sequestering of British property and provided that debts due from citizens of Virginia to British subjects would be paid directly into the treasury of the commonwealth and that such payments would operate to extinguish the debt. On April 26, 1780, the debtor Daniel Lawrence Hylton, acting in accordance with the Virginia act, paid into the treasury the amount owed his creditor, William Jones. Approximately one month later, on May 5, 1780, Hylton received a receipt, signed by "T. Jefferson," discharging him of his debt to Jones.

Following the war the estate administrator for Jones, John Tyndale Ware, filed suit in Virginia for recovery of the debt, based upon the wording of the peace treaty. Ware lost his case in the Virginia Circuit Court and appealed on error to the Supreme Court, enlisting William Lewis, Edward Tilghman, and John Wilcocks as his counsel. Lewis's opening statement declared that "individuals of different nations enter into contract with each other, upon a presumption, that, in case of a war, debts will not be confiscated." He explained that such a presumption was recognized by the monarchies of Europe and asserted that it would be in the best interests of the American republic to also recognize such a presumption as part of the modern law of nations—a law based upon practice rather than statute. Consequently, Lewis argued that a Virginia statute had no force in law if it conflicted with the modern law of nations. However, he acknowledged, as would the judges, that statute law did actually allow for confiscation of enemy debt by a foreign power. Lewis developed his argument around the question of Virginia's sovereignty and whether or not the commonwealth had a right to enact and execute such a sequestering law. Lewis posed three questions: did the Legislature of Virginia have competent authority to extinguish the debt? If the Legislature had such an authority, had it been exercised? And if the authority was lawfully exercised, what was the effect of the Treaty of Peace?

The first question grappled with the question of state sovereignty, the last with the extent of federal authority—opposite sides of the same issue. Lewis said, in essence, that the Virginia legislature had delegated their authority to Congress. Further, he argued that when war was declared against Britain, it was a war waged on behalf of America—as one nation—and that peace was concluded on the same principle. He stated that it would obviously be "absurd to suppose that Congress and Virginia could, at the same time, possess the powers of war and peace." He also maintained that Virginia was only one member of a belligerent sovereign body and, therefore, did not possess the right of confiscation independent of Congress. As a result, Lewis argued, the eminent domain of Virginia must be confined to internal affairs. In this particular case, internal affairs did not include jurisdiction over the debt owed by Hylton to Jones because Jones had resided in Britain, and, according to international law, debts are always due where a creditor resides.

Essentially, Lewis concluded that Virginia had no authority over the debt for two reasons, both of which confirmed the superiority of federal over state power and thus supported the Federalist view of America. First, Virginia was merely a member of a sovereign power, not a sovereign power unto itself.

Secondly, he reasoned, the peace treaty concluded by Congress after ratification of the Articles of Confederation must act upon all Americans equally. The particular portion of the treaty affecting the question of the debt owed by Hylton to Jones's estate stipulated, "It is agreed that creditors on either side shall meet with no lawful impediment to the recovery of the full value in sterling money of all bona fide debts heretofore contracted."

The Supreme Court, presided over by Justice Samuel Chase, ultimately found for Lewis's client Jones but, in the process, ignored Lewis's extreme nationalist argument denying Virginia's sovereignty. Instead, the court ruled that with the Declaration of Independence the states became sovereign and independent—therefore, Virginia had a right to enact the sequestration act of 1777. Additionally, the court ruled that any payments made under the act would be a legal bar to subsequent action upon the debt unless the creditor's right was revived by treaty, which, in the eyes of the court, it was. The court did agree that the treaty must act upon all Americans equally, citing the sixth article of the Constitution, which gives treaties the force of supreme law and which was interpreted as retroactive. Lastly, the court recognized the importance of the issue of the practice of modern law introduced by Lewis in his opening statements.[211]

An interesting footnote to *Ware v. Hylton* is that Lewis's opposition was the future chief justice, John Marshall. This was the one and only case Marshall ever argued before the Supreme Court—which he lost to William Lewis. As chief justice of the United States Supreme Court for thirty-five years, Marshall is credited for "giving meaning" to the Constitution—which he stated was the "work of the people, not the states." His appointment would be significant in that his influence would almost single-handedly reverse the tides that President Jefferson unleashed for state's rights upon *his* election in 1800.[212] In the Marshall court, it was the people who were sovereign, not the states. Lewis and Marshall would have been in full agreement on that.

Pemberton v. Hicks, Pennsylvania Supreme Court, December 1798:

Originally heard in the Bucks County Court of Common Pleas four years earlier, *Pemberton v. Hicks* would help set precedent in the state of Pennsylvania for those cases dealing with confiscated lands and property of those deemed either loyal to the British or lukewarm toward the Revolution. This case specifically involved a piece of property conveyed to Mr. Pemberton by the heirs of Grace Galloway. The property in question had been seized by the state when Joseph Galloway, Grace's husband, had been convicted and hanged for the crime of treason. Grace Galloway had disputed the seizure and sale of the particular lands that she had brought into the Galloway marriage (as separate from her husband's holdings). She made provisions in her will as to who would inherit the land, and upon her death in 1782 her heirs sold the land to Mr. Pemberton, who later leased the land to Richard Fenn. When Fenn sought to move onto the land in question, he was prevented from doing so by a Mr. Hicks, who had purchased the land in good faith from the state.

When the case reached the Pennsylvania Supreme Court, it was taken up by William Lewis and Edward Tilghman in defense of Pemberton and Jared Ingersoll and Alexander Dallas for Hicks. Lewis and Tilghman argued that once a child was brought into the marriage, the wife's estate did not belong to her husband in absolute and would not unless she preceded him in death. In their opinion, as Joseph Galloway was "killed civilly" by the state in 1778, the estate became the sole custody of Grace Galloway.

To Lewis and Tilghman, this was the only just answer. Ingersoll and Dallas argued the exact opposite—relying heavily on English common law precedents. They claimed that upon the birth of the Galloway daughter, Grace's lands had become the property of her husband. Before the judges ruled on the case, a new chief justice arrived to replace Justice McKean, who had just left the court to become the governor of the state. Luckily for Lewis and Tilghman, the views of Edward Shippen, McKean's replacement, would mirror their own. Shippen had attempted to remain neutral during the Revolution and was accused of being a Loyalist—and his infamous daughter Peggy Shippen had married Benedict Arnold. It was not surprising that the court ruled in favor of Pemberton. Their opinion was that, under certain conditions, a wife did not forfeit the lands and property she brought into the marriage as part of her dowry; accordingly, the wife did not forfeit the right to make the child her heir.[213]

The United States and French Privateering:

The bounds of the United States Constitution were most certainly being challenged daily as the government of our young nation was tested on a multitude of issues on many levels. How could the United States maintain a foreign policy of neutrality, ensure national security, and protect its own commercial interests while keeping peace at home? The executive, legislative, and judicial branches were quickly learning who should be playing in which field. The judiciary would step up during these years and play a significant role to ensure the proper implementation of policy as set forth by the legislature. Further, both the Washington and Adams administrations would rely heavily on the judicial branch to help maintain the appearance of United States neutrality and fairness. The "neutrality and fairness" of the judiciary is best illustrated by how French privateering cases were handled. While French diplomats attempted to lodge their complaints with senior United States cabinet members, they were told that these issues would be handled in the courts. Washington and his cabinet members were confident that the federal courts (as most of these cases ended up in the Supreme Court) would utilize the "law of nations," which did not merely regulate relations between nations—it conferred rights on private parties. They believed that ship owners, regardless of their nationalities, had a natural right to present their claims in court to defend their property rights. Additionally, these courts were able to properly scrutinize the large amounts of conflicting evidence that was necessary to adjudicate these matters.

Maritime law would become increasingly important and require ever more of William Lewis's focus. With no navy to protect the nation's commercial shipping trade, the Washington administration had signed the "Neutrality Proclamation" in 1793 in hopes of averting war with both France and Britain and keeping American goods flowing to overseas ports. Of course, neither France nor Britain was satisfied with this stance. Each preyed upon American shipping under the pretense of blocking shipments of wartime contraband to enemy ports. The war between France and the other European countries brought chaos especially on the high seas, where lawlessness was endemic.[214] Additionally, Great Britain continued to incite Indian attacks on frontier settlements where they maintained outposts. It seemed Hamilton's warning in the Federalist Papers now loomed as prophecy: "A nation, despicable by its weakness, forfeits even the privilege of being neutral."[215] The Washington administration was in a seemingly impossible situation.

Ironically, France—in desperate need to supplement their inadequate navy to continue their quest for trade disruption—would take further advantage of their position with the United States. France sent a new ambassador, Edmond Genet, to Charleston, South Carolina, with the specific task of commissioning U.S. citizens to act as privateers in the service of the French government. He also provided financial assistance to purchase and arm ships utilizing American ports. Further, Genet established "prize courts" in the major ports through French consuls. As a result, "French" privateers began bringing their prizes (captured ships and cargo) into U.S. ports so that French consuls could adjudicate the lawfulness of their prizes. Of course, Washington viewed Genet's efforts as a flagrant violation of America's neutrality stance, and he quickly requested a recall of this ambassador, which was granted.

Congress found their earlier regulation from the year prior had been insufficient in preventing the French from operating in American ports, so in June of 1794 they removed all doubts by authorizing criminal punishment.[216] The new legislation expressly authorized criminal penalties for U.S. citizens who "accept[ed] and exercise[d] a commission to serve a foreign prince or state in war [or who] enlisted or entered in the service of any foreign prince or state . . . as a marine or seaman on board of any vessel of war . . . or privateer." Additionally, the legislation included three provisions to address the problem of illegal outfitting in U.S. ports. First, the statute made it a crime for any person within U.S. territory to "fit out and arm . . . any ship or vessel with intent that such ship or vessel shall be employed in the service of any foreign prince or state to cruise or commit hostilities upon the subjects, citizens or property of another foreign prince or state with whom the United States are at peace." The statute imposed similar penalties for anyone who augmented or increased "the force of any ship of war, cruiser or other armed vessel" in the service of a foreign state that was at war with a state "with whom the United States are at peace, by adding to the number or size of the guns of such vessel." Additionally, the statute authorized the President to detain any vessel that had been illegally outfitted, or whose force had been illegally augmented, in a U.S. port.[217]

Between February 1794 and February 1797, the U.S. Supreme Court decided twenty-four cases arising from French privateering activities, including fourteen published decisions and ten unpublished decisions. These cases accounted for roughly half of the Supreme Court caseload during this period—a substantial portion.[218]

Taking full advantage of the American judicial system, Benjamin Moodie, the British consul in South Carolina, alone filed eleven cases seeking restitution of British merchant vessels captured by French privateers. Even though he eventually lost most of his cases, he was quite satisfied with the results, as the courts typically retained custody of the captured property (or the funds from sale of the property) for twelve to eighteen months while judicial proceedings were pending—just enough time to wreak havoc on the French privateers' plundering plans. Additionally, since Charleston was where privateers routinely brought their prizes, it would also be the leading venue for these admiralty actions, as cases were filed where the ship was located.

Of the twenty-four French privateering cases in the U.S. Supreme Court, William Lewis would be directly involved in nine of them, both published and unpublished.

Published Cases:
> *Hill v. Ross*, 3 U.S. (3 Dallas p. 184)
> *Del Col v. Arnold*, 3 U.S. (3 Dallas p. 333)
> *Cotton v. Wallace*, 3 U.S. (3 Dallas p. 302)
> *Geyer v. Michel*, 3 U.S. (3 Dallas p. 285)

Moodie v. Ship Betty Cathcart, 3 U.S. (3 Dallas p. 285)
Talbot v. Janson, 3 U.S. (3 Dallas p. 133)

Unpublished Cases:

Wallace v. Brig Caesar, Supreme Court Case #11
Moodie v. Ship Mermaid, Supreme Court Case #17
Moodie v. Brig Favorite, Supreme Court Case #22

In general, these French privateering cases touched upon treaties, commerce, and actions of an individual, especially as they were bound by a country's treaties with other nations. Lewis's second-most-cited case, *Talbot v. Janson*, is a useful illustration of the issues Lewis dealt with in these privateering cases.[219]

Talbot v. Janson, U.S. Supreme Court, 1795:

Talbot v. Janson rose to the Supreme Court on appeal from the Circuit Court of South Carolina and dealt with the issues outlined above. It also helped define the process of lawful expatriation. The rulings in the Talbot case supported free commerce by confirming the superiority of a federal treaty over the operation of state law and by upholding obligations of a neutral power dealing with belligerent nations. The case was complicated. It involved three ships, three captains, and three countries. The countries: the warring nations of France and the Netherlands and the neutral United States. The ships: *L'Ami de la Liberté*, captained by Edward Ballard, *L'Ami de la Point à Petre*, captained by William Talbot, and the *Magdalena*, captained by Joost Janson.[220]

On May 16, 1794, the Dutch brigantine *Magdalena*, on a voyage from Curacao to Amsterdam, was captured and taken as prize of war by Captain Ballard of the French vessel *L'Ami de la Liberté*. The following day, Captain Talbot of the French ship *L'Ami de la Point à Petre* boarded the *Magdalena*, assumed command and arranged for the *Magdelena* to sail to Charleston. The case centered on the nationalities of Ballard and Talbot, both Americans who claimed expatriation and French citizenship. Lewis, representing Janson of the *Magdalena*, argued that neither Ballard nor Talbot had actually satisfied the legalities of expatriation and were therefore bound as American citizens by the treaty existing between the United States and the Netherlands as well as by the general law of neutrality and the law of nations. Beyond the question of the nationality of each captain, there were questions regarding jurisdiction of the circuit court and the vessel themselves, their construction, outfitting, and ownership—all purportedly American.

Counsel for Talbot—the prominent Philadelphia lawyers Ingersoll, Dallas and Du Ponceau—detailed at great length the evolution of the rights, obligations, and requirements of citizenship throughout recorded time. In their final analysis they argued that Talbot and Ballard's acceptance of a French commission for privateering, coupled with their declarations of expatriation, were sufficient proofs that they were no longer American citizens. Lewis, citing international authorities, argued that neither had left the country under the regulations prescribed by law, nor had they established residency in France or French territory. Ballard had never even sailed into a non-American port. Lewis also maintained that a person's reception as a citizen of another country did not mean that one's own country had surrendered him—therefore, that person was still bound by the laws of his original country.

Lewis claimed the importance of restraint in expatriation, reasoning that it could not be exercised in "contravention of a national compact, such as the American treaty with Holland . . . or to the injury of the emigrant's country." He further asserted that if the actions of Talbot and Ballard were considered legal, others would adopt the same strategy for the same financial rewards, and then "we might behold a political monster, all the citizens of a country at war though the country itself is at peace."[221] Lewis also insisted that the Virginia act cited by Ballard as the law governing his expatriation had no authority because "the power of regulating emigration is an incident to the power of regulating naturalization," and such a power is "vested exclusively in Congress." Lewis further argued that the jurisdictional power of the circuit courts in Admiralty cases was well established and that in this case nothing in either the law of nations or the treaty with France prevented American judicial authority.

The court, presided over by Chief Justice Edward Rutledge, agreed that the Virginia law had no effect on United States citizenship. Justice Samuel Patterson's opinion addressed the question of expatriation, noting Ballard's failure to even visit a foreign port, much less establish a residency elsewhere, suggested that "perchance he should be a citizen of the world . . . such a character bespeaks universal benevolence and breathes peace on earth and good will to man, it forbids roving on the ocean in quest of plunder."[222]

The court found for Lewis's client Janson, commenting on the necessity of establishing expatriation by an internationally recognized process. The justices also condemned the prize capture as illegal because the French registered vessels of Ballard and Talbot were in actuality owned by American citizens and had been outfitted with American stores in American waters—all of which were in violation of both international neutrality laws and of an American treaty with Holland. On the question of jurisdiction, the court held that "all piracies and trespasses committed against the general law of nations are inquirable, and may be proceeded against in any nation."[223]

The outcome of *Talbot v. Janson* operated to protect the commerce of nations from the unscrupulous acts of would-be legal pirates on the high seas. Lewis's successful arguments in this case and the others were key in establishing protection for American commercial interests. The actions in the United States courts—aided by the Jay Treaty and geopolitical developments in the Caribbean—had such an impact that by early November 1795, French privateering activities in U.S. ports had all but ceased.[224]

Not surprisingly, Washington also signed legislation authorizing the construction of six heavy frigates—larger and more powerful than a sloop, yet smaller, lighter, and faster than a battleship—to be built at the six major seaports.[225] While Britain alone had hundreds of powerful warships, this piece of legislation would become the start of the American navy.

In an attempt to face the British issues head on, Secretary of State Hamilton, with strong support from Washington and chief negotiator John Jay, was working on a British treaty. Ultimately, the agreement between the United States and Britain would avert war, solve the residual issues left over from the Revolution, and result in a decade of peaceful trade amidst the French Revolutionary wars. Needless to say, this was a hotly contested issue. Despite efforts by Jefferson and his fellow Democratic-Republicans to defeat it, the Jay Treaty was ratified by Congress. Signed in November of 1794, it did not officially take effect until February 29, 1796. The British would finally withdraw from their occupied posts in the Northwest Territories, and both wartime debts and the United States-Canadian boundary would finally be addressed. Additionally, Article 24 of the Jay Treaty expressly prohibited privateers commissioned by France from selling their prizes in U.S. ports as long as France was at war with Great Britain.

To the consternation of the pro-French Republicans—who believed that the Jay Treaty was a Federalist attack on the Republican merchants who traded with France—United States and French relations continued to fall apart. Diplomatic relations would come to a head after John Adams became president in 1797. Despite the Adams administration's best efforts, the French directory refused to deal with the American commissioners sent to France without first being paid a substantial bribe. The insult to the American delegation became known as the "XYZ Affair" in reference to the Congressional report on the subject which referred to the specific Frenchmen involved only as "X," "Y," and "Z." An undeclared "Quasi-War" between the two countries resulted in each country attacking and capturing the other's ships.

Public sentiments against the French ran high, Adams benefitted from the good tidings, and the Federalists were able to expand the navy and enlarge the army. To pay for national security, in July 1798 the Congress imposed two million dollars in new taxes on real estate, buildings, and slaves, apportioned among the states. Goodwill towards the Federalists would disappear as the public grew unruly. In Pennsylvania, the Fries Rebellion broke out—an armed revolt among Pennsylvania farmers of German descent. The Fries Rebellion was actually the third tax-related rebellion, the earlier two being Shays's Rebellion and the Whiskey Rebellion.

The Whiskey Rebellion Treason Law Case: United States v. the Insurgents of Pennsylvania

The Whiskey Rebellion was set off by an excise tax on tobacco, sugar, and whiskey products imposed in 1794, the proceeds of which would help establish Hamilton's plan for government operating capital. In western Pennsylvania, the turmoil surrounding the excise tax would come to a head after William Rawle, then federal district attorney, issued subpoenas for more than sixty distillers who had not paid their taxes. By August, Justice James Wilson would declare that western Pennsylvania was in a state of rebellion, and President Washington soon followed with a proclamation announcing that the militia would be called in to suppress it.[226] By the time Washington sent out fifteen thousand troops, the insurrection had already collapsed. Jefferson wrote to Madison at the end of December 1794, "The excise law is an infernal one. The information of our militia, returned from Westward, is uniform, that the people there let them pass quietly; they were objects of their laughter, not their fear."[227] Approximately twenty people were arrested and marched to Philadelphia, where some were released on bail and others detained while awaiting trial. Lewis's well-established reputation as a treason lawyer likely signaled him out as the best chance for the accused.[228] By agreeing to defend these insurgents in court, Lewis was not only putting his belief in individual rights over his political views, he was directly challenging the Federalist authorities. His first act on their behalf was to move for the establishment of special courts in the western counties of Pennsylvania, where the offenses were committed. The motion would be denied, and the trials would open in the United States District Court in Philadelphia in May of 1795. These cases would be the first treason cases brought to court since the adoption of the United States Constitution. Lewis would use this fact to remind the court of their imperative to "prevent the introduction of precedents, injurious to the rights and safety of posterity."[229] With this in mind, Lewis would defend the rights of the accused by highlighting issues such as the fact that jury members from eastern Pennsylvania were sitting in judgment of western frontiersmen as well as the need to allot time for summons of a witness from the western counties and the corresponding travel time of said witness. Several of the defendants were indeed found guilty, but they were eventually pardoned by Washington.

Fries Rebellion Treason Law Case: United States v. John Fries

The Fries Rebellion, the second Pennsylvania protest against taxes, was led by local Revolutionary War hero John Fries. A skirmish with local militia ensued, but no weapons were fired. The band freed their neighbors who were being held for not paying their taxes. Fries was ultimately charged with treason. This rebellion and others like it illustrated a growing resistance movement in the western and southern parts of the country, with many farmers not only refusing to pay their taxes but openly attacking the agents sent to collect them. As tensions grew, farmers joined the artisans and tradesman in identifying the Federalists as aristocrats and continued to join the cause of the Democratic-Republicans.

John Fries, arrested and charged with treason against the United States for his actions as the leader of insurrection protesting the land tax imposed by Congress, would go to trial in Philadelphia in 1799 in front of Judge Richard Peters of the United States District Court for the District of Pennsylvania and Justice James Iredell of the United States Supreme Court. Beyond the fact that a man's life was on the line, the trial and its players would be subject to a number of remarkable proceedings—dueling co-counsel, a prejudiced juror, a change in venue, and even a verdict handed down before the lawyers presented their case—all of which would have unanticipated repercussions for years to come. In the end, the trial was about more than treason; it helped to set a precedent for what a "fair" trial would look like.

A group of Fries's sympathizers hired two lawyers to represent him at trial. Of course it would be no surprise that they would hire the celebrated treason defender William Lewis. What was unusual was that they hired William Lewis, the epitome of all that was Federalist, along with Alexander J. Dallas, a man who represented the opposite side of the coin. Lewis, who preferred not to share a case with equal co-counsel—let alone with someone he greatly disliked—was unaware when he agreed to take on the case that Dallas would be his colleague. Lewis so antagonized Dallas that he ended up challenging Lewis to a duel.[230] William Rawle, the district attorney on the case, intervened—smoothing over the anger and friction. With the duel set aside, Lewis and Dallas actually worked together quite well in their defense of Fries. Unfortunately, their defense was not enough, and Fries was convicted. Lewis, however, was able to prove that the jury had been prejudiced by proving that one of its members had publicly declared—before the trial—that Fries should be hanged.[231] Fries was granted a new trial.

The second trial was held in April 1800 with Maryland Supreme Court Justice Samuel Chase and United States District Court Judge Richard Peters presiding. Immediately upon the jury being sworn in, contrary to normal procedure—and without having heard any portion of the case—Judge Chase submitted in writing "the law" as he intended to lay it down in his charge to the jury. Judge Peters, knowing perfectly well what the reaction would be, attempted a protest, but, nevertheless, Judge Chase handed down his opinion to Lewis. Lewis refused to receive it, declaring, "My hand should never be tainted by the touch of a paper containing a prejudged opinion in any case . . . much less a capital one."[232] In spite of his embarrassment, the judge persisted, causing Lewis and Dallas to withdraw from the defense. Lewis's response was generally viewed as an assertion of the rights of counsel, and by extension, the rights of both the accused and the jury. The departure of Fries's counsel left Rawle, as district attorney, to prosecute Fries. Rawle wanted no part of condemning an undefended man to death by hanging—which was the final verdict.

Immense controversy ensued, and on May 21, President John Adams pardoned Fries and two other convicted insurgents, as well as all the other prisoners found guilty of opposing the government tax. While Adams was a bit vague about his reasoning, the pardon was due in part to a letter written by Lewis to the president in which he explained the tack he would have taken had he stayed with the case in the court. As for the infamous Justice Samuel Chase, he would face impeachment in 1805. Among the myriad of complaints filed against him was "his alleged misconduct in the second trial of John Fries."[233]

Traveling the Judicial Circuit

William Lewis would continue to try cases throughout the eastern states. By 1801, when the United States Supreme Court moved south with the rest of the federal government, he became a frequent traveler to Washington, D.C. The Philadelphia lawyers—even those representing opposing parties—traveled together, sharing the expense of carriages and lodging along the way. Upon arrival at their destination, there was great pride in being part of the Philadelphia bar, as these lawyers had earned great respect among their peers. Lewis's former student Peter Du Ponceau recalled how it felt to appear before the Supreme Court: "Our appearance at the bar of the Supreme Court was always a scene of triumph. We entered the hall together, and Judge Bushrod Washington [a former Philadelphia lawyer] was heard to say, 'This is *my* bar.' . . . It was really a proud thing at that time to be a *Philadelphia lawyer.*"[234]

Serving as a justice on the early Supreme Court was not glamorous; in fact it could actually be dangerous duty. Back in 1789, a judiciary act authored by Oliver Ellsworth compelled Supreme Court Justices to ride around the country attending circuit courts. Maeva Marcus explains:

> The Justices detested their circuit duties and spent much time lobbying Congress to change the system. Attending circuit courts twice a year in several states in addition to two sessions of the Supreme Court at the seat of government kept the Justices away from home for the better part of the year. Traveling to the Supreme Court in the two worst months of the year, February and August, and then great distances in the spring and fall over bumpy, muddy roads or trails did not add to the glamour of the job.[235]

Nor did the Justices enjoy the accommodations along the way. Occasionally they would visit with friends, but more often the justices lodged at taverns, where the crowded and uncomfortable sleeping conditions, coupled with the noise from below, did little to provide relief from the tiring journey. And while at first a justice might feel his salary made the travel worthwhile, once the expenses for traveling the circuit were calculated, there was very little money left when the year was over. The Supreme Court justices may not have minded that when they met in Philadelphia for the first decade that they shared space with the Pennsylvania courts. They certainly would not have been happy, however, to discover when they got to Washington that they had been forgotten and no accommodations had been arranged for them.[236] While awaiting their own building, Congress allowed them to use a small basement room in the unfinished Capitol building.

Of course, what was true for the justices was also true for the counselors, who would likewise travel to multiple locations. Sharing accommodations with one's fellow travelers would certainly provide moments of discomfort. Horace Binney described what it was like to share a room with Lewis . . . and his ever-present cigars.

> He smoked cigars incessantly. He smoked at the fireplace in Court. He smoked in the Court Library. He smoked in his office. He smoked in the street. He smoked in bed; and he would have smoked in church . . . if he had ever gone there. . . . The smoking in bed was, in one instance, literally verified by myself and my venerable master, upon a winter journey to the Supreme Court at Washington, in the year 1809, when, in the days of coaching, we passed our first night at the Head of Elk; and I called Mr. Ingersoll's attention to it, after we had got into our respective beds in the same large room, and the last candle had been extinguished. The cigar was then seen firing up from Mr. Lewis's pillow, and disappearing in the darkness, like a revolving light on the coast.[237]

William Rawle, self-portrait with Lewis smoking "Segars."
Journals of William Rawle, Sr., Rawle Family Papers,
Historical Society of Pennsylvania.

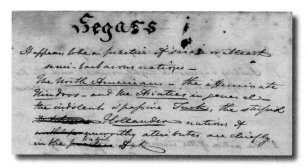

William Rawle, "Segars" disquisition. Journals
of William Rawle, Sr., Rawle Family Papers,
Historical Society of Pennsylvania.

One of William Rawle's journal entries features a sketch he drew of himself and his good friend Lewis enjoying a smoke. Smoking was such an important part of their social life that Rawle was inspired to write a disquisition about the perils of smoking entitled "Segars" in his journal. According to Rawle, the "moral objections [to smoking] are many & weighty," and when a person partakes in the practice he experiences a "temporary torpor of the mind" while fixated on the ministrations of the "segar" to such a degree that it "debilitates conversation." We assume that Rawle had tongue in cheek when he stated that smoking was more a practice of the savages and not practiced by the better people, especially the Greeks and Romans.[238]

While second-hand smoke certainly wasn't good for your health, traveling to and from the United States Supreme Court via carriage could literally mean putting your life at risk. Peter Du Ponceau recollected the tribulations of one such trip in a letter to Thomas Wharton:

In the beginning of the present [nineteenth] century, during the reign of the embargo, non-intercourse, and other restrictive measures . . . a great number of causes were carried from this city to the Supreme Court of the United States. The counsel engaged in those causes were in the habit of going together to Washington, to argue their cases before that tribunal. These were Mr. Ingersoll, Mr. Dallas, Mr. Lewis, Mr. Edward Tilghman, Mr. Rawle and myself. . . . We hired a stage to ourselves. . . . We had to travel in the depth of winter, through bad roads, in the midst of rain, hail and snow, in no very comfortable way. Nevertheless, as soon as we were out of the city, and felt the flush of air, we were like school boys on the play ground on a holiday; and we began to kill time by all the means that our imagination could suggest. Flashes of wit . . . and puns of the genuine Philadelphia stamp were handed about; old college stories were revived; macaronic Latin was spoken with great purity; songs were sung . . . in short, we might have been taken for anything but the grave counselors of the celebrated bar of Philadelphia. We returned home of course, in the same manner that we had proceeded to the capitol. We occasionally met with accidents in going or returning, but none worth relating, except the one that I am about to mention. On our way to Baltimore, we were all in very high spirits. . . . To such a degree was our mirth carried, that our Irish driver, listening to us, did not perceive a stump before him; the carriage made a terrible jolt, our Phaeton was thrown from his seat, the horses took fright and ran away with us at a dreadful rate . . . with a creek before us. . . . It was determined to jump out of the carriage . . . . I collected all my presence of mind . . . and jumped out so fortunately, that I fell upon my feet without the least injury. Turning back to look behind me, the first thing I saw was my friend Lewis, sprawling upon the ground. . . . I raised him on his feet, and presently came our companions, more or less bruised. . . . We all determined to walk to Baltimore as well as we could . . . when to our great comfort we saw our stage returning, under safe guidance. . . . We joyfully resumed our places [and by] the next day resumed our route towards Philadelphia. We had a narrow escape.[239]

Receipt from the Indian Queen Tavern, c. 1810, a place frequented by Lewis on his trips to the United States Supreme Court. Lewis family papers.

Nineteen days before the end of Adams's days as president and twelve years after the establishment of the federal judiciary, Congress approved a sweeping reorganization of the nation's court system and significantly expanded federal jurisdiction. The Judiciary Act of 1801, also known as "An Act to provide for the more convenient organization of the Courts of the United States" was passed on February 13, 1801. The act reduced the size of the Supreme Court from six justices to five and eliminated the justices' circuit duties. To replace the justices on circuit, the act created sixteen judgeships for six judicial circuits.

The U.S. circuit courts over which the new judges would preside gained jurisdiction over all cases arising under the Constitution and acts of the United States. The division of states to create additional circuit and district courts further encouraged citizens to rely on the federal rather than state courts. Overall, the act allowed the Supreme Court greater power and control over the cases. Additionally, President Adams filled several of the new judgeships before he left office, leaving many Republicans feeling that he had "loaded the courts" with Federalists, including Chief Justice John Marshall.

War on the Judiciary: Federalists v. Republicans

Jefferson's viewpoint when he became president in March of 1801 was that thanks to Washington and Adams, he had inherited a system of circuit courts—created by a Federalist-controlled Congress—presided over by the individual justices of the Supreme Court, all of whom were Federalists in 1800. Most of the lower judges on the circuit also affiliated themselves with the Federalists. Additionally, Jefferson found that by decreasing the number of Supreme Court justices from six to five through the Judiciary Act, the lame-duck Federalist Congress had effectively limited his ability to make Republican appointments. Jefferson also deemed that the new system of circuit courts was filled with Federalist judges, attorneys, clerks, and marshals. Secretary of State James Madison decided to refuse delivery of any of Adams's judicial commissions, put forth before he left office, in hopes of keeping some of the new Federalist judges off the bench. However, Jefferson was powerless to simply dismiss the current judges, because they were appointed for life. But he did replace most of the marshals and other court officers with Republicans. Still, the Federalist-dominated Supreme Court, with justices who were appointed for life and who were led by the recently appointed Chief Justice John Marshall, still remained—much to the consternation of Jefferson and his fellow Republicans.[240] This was especially so as Jefferson had eagerly anticipated appointing a new chief justice and was angered to learn that Adams had rushed to beat him to it. Jefferson remained wary that the federal judiciary had too much power.

As soon as possible, the Jefferson administration proposed a bill to repeal the Judiciary Act of 1801. While the bill was in the United States Senate, the members of the Philadelphia bar attempted to sway opinion. On January 29, 1802, they submitted a petition to the U.S. Senate in response to the circuit court change. William Lewis would be active in this petition, becoming one of its thirty-two signers. The bar hoped to remind the senators what was at stake with their repeal of the Judiciary Act of 1801:

> To the Honorable Senate of the United States.
>
> The subscribers, counselors practicing in the courts of Pennsylvania, and in the Circuit Courts of the United States for the eastern district of Pennsylvania, respectfully represent,
>
> That they do not conceive it consistent with their professional duty, to remain silent observers of a bill, now pending before the Senate of the United States, entitled "A bill to repeal certain acts respecting the organization of the courts of the United States, and for other purposes."
>
> That they do not, however, undertake to express an opinion to the Legislature of the Union, on questions of constitutional or political nature; but confine their representation to facts, upon the nature and extent of which, they hope that they may

be deemed competent to give information.

That under the former law, the greatest inconveniences were experienced by the courts, by the bar, and by the Jurors. The judges were constantly employed in traversing the several states, with little opportunity for reflecting or repose.

The same judges who saw the origin of suit, or who gave the interlocutory orders in its progress, seldom pronounced the final decision. Judges presided in states, the laws, usages and practice of which, were essentially different from the laws, usages, and practice of the States in which they were respectively educated, and without adverting to the casualties of indisposition and of weather, the inevitable consequences of the late system, were embarrassment, uncertainty, and delay.

That although the members of the Bar of Philadelphia may be supposed to differ in their political sentiment they unanimously concur, in testifying the sense they entertain of the great abilities, learning and integrity of the gentlemen, who at present fill the offices of judges of the circuit court of the United States, for the third circuit. The sense of business has already been extensive beyond all anticipation and the increasing confidence of the public, as well as of the profession, promises to render the court an honor and a benefit to the nation. Causes of the greatest interest have been heard with exemplary patience and candor; have been decided with caution and firmness; and the foreigner as well as the citizen, had received an ample assurance of the prompt and unpartial administration of justice.

In the state courts, indeed, although filled by gentlemen, in whose talents, learning and integrity, equal confidence is deservedly placed, and whose patience, candor, caution and firmness are equally displayed, so many sons are depending that a speedy termination of causes is no longer in that quarter to be expected.

That under these impressions, as public and professional characters, the subscribers respectfully submit their unanimous opinion, deliberately and anxiously formed, that the circuit court, on the principles of its present organization, is an important medium, for the administration of justice, and that the abolition of the court, will probably be attended with great public inconvenience. "

/s/ Moses Levy, Samuel Levy, Wm. Meredith, John R. Smith, C. W. Hare, Bird Wilson, James Gibson, W. Sergeant, J. Sergeant, H. Binney, C. Read, Joseph Reed, Thomas B. Ankinsey, J.H. Brinton, Peter S. Du Ponceau, Jared Ingersoll, Edward Tilghman, William Lewis, W. Rawle, Charles Heatly, A.J. Dallas, Jos. B. McKean, Charles Swift, Benjamin R. Morgan, John Hallowell, Joseph Hopkinson, W. H. Todd, J.W. Condy, Miers Fisher, J.B. Wallace, Charles Chanddes, Wal. Franklin.[241]

Despite the best efforts of the leaders of the Philadelphia bar and the constitutional concept of an independent judiciary, the Judiciary Act of 1801 was, indeed, repealed. Jefferson continued to use his power to further undermine and weaken the power of the judiciary, with his ultimate target being the Supreme Court. Two impeachment proceedings were initiated to test the waters for removal of the Federalist justices by trial. According to the U.S. Constitution, a federal judge can be removed from office only for "high crimes and misdemeanors." In the first test, Justice John Pickering, a highly partisan Federalist who was also an alcoholic and perhaps in an advanced stage of senility, was tried by the Senate based upon articles of impeachment drawn up by the House. Pickering was removed from office by a strict party vote. A blow had been struck. Jefferson was successful in illustrating the vulnerability of the federal judiciary to the impeachment power of Congress.[242]

The next assault on the federal judiciary was the impeachment of Justice Samuel Chase, an able but nearly fanatic anti-Jeffersonian who frequently delivered streams of abuse from the bench. Fortunately for Chase, he had defenders among moderate Republicans in the Senate who feared overreaching their congressional authority. In the latter case, the Senate vote failed to carry the two-thirds majority in favor of conviction. Chase was safe.

The impeachment trial of Justice Chase had to be particularly perplexing for William Lewis. He certainly would have viewed Jefferson's actions as overreaching. And as illustrated in his signature on the Philadelphia bar petition, Lewis heartily believed in the changes the Judiciary Act of 1801 allowed. Regardless of his Federalist beliefs, he believed first and foremost in a person's right to a speedy and fair trial. This, of course, had been his precise complaint against Judge Chase several years before, when Chase had attempted to hand down his decision at the start of the second Fries trial. Lewis might have agreed that Chase should be impeached, but not for Jefferson's political gain.

Although Jefferson did manage to repeal the Judiciary Act of 1801 and thus dismiss many Federalist judges, his efforts to get Chase impeached had failed. The Supreme Court, led by Chief Justice John Marshall, would carve out a unique and powerful role as the protector of the Constitution. Marshall is given credit for setting precedent to give the Supreme Court power to declare acts of Congress—or the president—invalid if contrary to the Constitution. Jefferson sincerely and bitterly opposed the idea that any court, including the Supreme Court, had the power to declare an act of the Congress unconstitutional. [243]

Men like William Lewis believed in the proper balance of powers. And while Lewis was an ardent Federalist, he put his political beliefs aside when he entered the courtroom. The respect Lewis gained as the "most celebrated lawyer in Philadelphia" came directly from the respect he gave to the judiciary process.[244] Integrity mattered above all else. This is the impression David Paul Brown shared in his writings:

> The true dignity and harmony of courts of justice, depend upon a just observance of the relative position of court and counsel; mutual respect for each other, or—if I may say so—"taking and giving odor." I have seen the Judges of the Supreme Court, in its most palmy state, before the hour of taking their seats, engaged in a friendly and sprightly conversation with a knot of the members of the bar, upon the most agreeable, familiar, and equal terms; but the moment they assumed their places, conversation ended, and business commenced. There was no longer any familiarity, though always great courtesy, great kindness, and great attention.[245]

The Aaron Burr Treason Law Case

Perhaps the ultimate illustration of integrity and Lewis's ability to put personal and political differences aside in the cause of justice was his involvement in the trial of Aaron Burr in 1807. Burr was not a well-liked man and certainly would not have been a friend of Lewis. The infamous July 1804 duel between Burr and Hamilton and Hamilton's subsequent death caught the nation by surprise. Hamilton's supporters were heartbroken—Lewis included—and took to wearing black crepe armbands in his honor. The observations of the Reverend Dr. Mason of New York as reported in the *American Daily Advertiser* on August, 2, 1804, captured the prevailing sentiments of the country:

> Your tears may well mingle with the blood of ALEXANDER HAMILTON. Great God! when WASHINGTON dies, we had HAMILTON left; but HAMILTON is dead, and we have no WASHINGTON![246]

The villainous Burr had immediately left town after the duel, heading west on a reconnaissance mission through the newly acquired Louisiana Territory—a place with growing boundary tensions between Spain, Mexico, and the native Indians. During his trip, Burr was captured and accused of attempting to build a coalition to capture New Orleans and create a new western empire independent of the United States. In May of 1807, Burr was brought to trial in Richmond, Virginia with Chief Justice John Marshall presiding. Burr was indicted for treason and high misdemeanors and was represented by his original counsel of five attorneys. The debate continued with both the prosecution and the defense arguing over the evidence. On August 17, newspapers announced, "the celebrated William Lewis, of Philadelphia, is added to the number of Colonel Burr's counsel."[247] Three days later the tone of the trial changed, as the defense moved that the prosecution had "utterly failed to prove an overt act of war," which is how the Constitution very specifically defines treason. Several weeks of debate followed, and the case ended in early September. The jury found Burr not guilty of treason as defined by the Constitution. It is fascinating to ponder the effect William Lewis had on this seminal case in United States treason law more than twenty-five years after he had helped to establish the precedents in these types of cases. No one knew treason law better than Lewis, and when called upon, he was willing to use his expertise to free the man who had killed his friend.

Lewis's Late Legal Career

William Lewis never completely retired from the practice of law. There are indications that he did cut back on his caseload by withdrawing from certain types of cases such as criminal practice.[248] According to Binney, even in his last years, Lewis never doubted his intellectual powers, even when he was less than prepared for court. His office was known to be in a constant state of disarray—a nightmare to those who worked within and who might be called upon to find a particular file. And he often confounded the bench by holding up a trial to buy more time for preparation, even using his health as cause for delay.[249] Yet Lewis could always be counted on to come to the aid of a friend or trusted associate, as when he agreed to represent the Bank of North America in a suit against a counterfeiter. Lewis stated his gratitude to the bank for having hired him as a counselor in his younger days, which prevented him from turning down their request for aid in his old age. He had been a counselor for the bank for more than twenty years. According to Brown's story, the lawyer for the counterfeiter (not a particularly handsome man), used the fact that his client was a man of considerable attraction as a means for defense. In his conclusion, the opposing lawyer exhorted, "Do you think, gentlemen of the jury . . . that *such* a man could be capable of perpetrating *such* an offense? Can you suppose that so calm and fair a countenance could mantle over so false and foul a heart?" Lewis's characteristic withering sarcasm was on full display as he rose to reply, "the prisoner's counsel has placed his defense mainly upon his countenance. What does such reliance result in? If a good countenance is to pass for an acquittal, a bad countenance must pass for a condemnation; doctrine that you will at once object, for in the case, [pointing to opposing counsel] he himself would stand a wretchedly poor chance."[250] As always, Lewis could be counted upon to point out the logic that could not be denied.

The very last case Lewis tried came in the spring of 1819 in the Pennsylvania state court. The case was *Willing v. Tilghman*, with Lewis representing Willing and Horace Binney representing Chief Justice Tilghman. According to Binney, Tilghman—Lewis's contemporary at the bar—was anxious for a quick trial and had expected Lewis's "now very usual effort for procrastination." As predicted, in the course of Lewis's reply, he became faint and sat down, but he soon recovered and went on speaking.[251] On this occasion, however, it seems his indisposition was sincere, for that was the last time he was ever seen in court. Lewis's health prevented his return.

Seven

How are The Mighty Fallen:

The Death of William Lewis

William Lewis's lifetime of heavy smoking had taken a toll on his health in later years as he suffered the effects of what was most likely emphysema. He did not slow down until the very end, continuing to practice law and agitate for those causes he had always supported. He served as senior counselor at the Pennsylvania bar until his health prevented him from returning to court. The last few months of his life were spent at Summerville, his country retreat. Perhaps the beautiful view of the Schuylkill River as it flowed quietly past his property provided some sense of comfort as he pondered a life well spent. Lewis died at home on August 16, 1819.

The next morning the following announcement appeared in *Poulson's American Daily Advertiser*:

> Died, yesterday morning, after a lingering illness, in the sixty-ninth year of his age, WILLIAM LEWIS, Esquire, Counsellor at Law.
>
> His friends are invited to attend his Funeral at 10 o'clock this morning, from his late residence on the Ridge Road, to St. Peter's Church.[252]

Formal invitations were also delivered to invitees. Curiously, the Lewis's estate papers included one such invitation, perhaps returned by the recipient upon his appearance at the funeral—it is hand-addressed to "Relations of Wm Lewis, deceased," with the specific name "Stephan Girard, Esq."[253]

While the specifics of their relationship are unknown, the paths of Lewis and Girard would have crossed often, whether on opposite sides of the political spectrum or in matters of trade and commerce. This particular invitation is indicative of the fact that Lewis's funeral procession included a wide cross-section of attendees, from the well known to the common man.

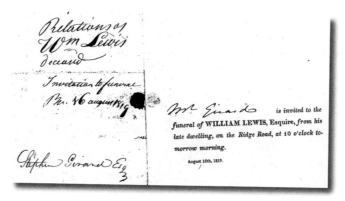

Stephen Girard's invitation to Lewis's funeral. Lewis family papers.

The procession met at Summerville and then traveled to St. Peter's Church at Third and Pine Streets for the funeral service and burial. We do not know the exact location of Lewis's remains within the cemetery as his headstone no longer exists.[254]

Among the many disintegrated headstones in the cemetery at St. Peter's Church, Lewis remains in the company of his well-known compatriots Nicholas Biddle, Benjamin Chew, and Charles Willson Peale.

Among the tributes for Lewis was one called by the Philadelphia Bar. The group, led by chair Jared Ingersoll, met in the Supreme Court Room on August 18 to forward a resolution that "as a mark of respect for the memory of William Lewis, Esquire, the Members of this Bar will wear crape on their left arm for the space of thirty days from this date."[255] Offered by Peter Du Ponceau and seconded by Meredith, the resolution was unanimously adopted.

Two obituaries were printed within a few days after Lewis's death. Both were written by Major William Jackson, Lewis's former law student and good friend. The original handwritten drafts were found among the Lewis estate papers in Wilkes-Barre, Pennsylvania. The first obituary was printed in *Poulson's The American Daily Advertiser* on Thursday morning, August 19:

WILLIAM LEWIS, Esquire.

How are the mighty fallen! I repeated to myself as I read the notice of the death of this great man. Tell it not in Georgia—publish it not in the plains of Virginia—for Lewis was the friend of Black Men. A statesman of the Revolution, jealous of liberty himself, he wished its enjoyment to all; and while many around him were trafficking in their fellowmen, Lewis was engaged in breaking their shackles asunder—long may the citizens of Pennsylvania hold his memory in reverence, as an enlightened Statesman—a profound Lawyer—and a useful Citizen—and to few is the state indebted more than to William Lewis for her freedom from that diabolical crime of holding part of her Citizens in Slavery to the rest. As a member of the Legislature—as a Lawyer—as a Citizen—he employed all his influence to effect that object.

The cases in which he was concerned to protect the Africans from bondage are too many to enumerate—they would fill a volume.

"When the ear heard him, then it blessed him, and when the eye saw him it gave witness to him, because he delivered the poor that cried and the fatherless, and him that had none to help him—the blessing of him that was ready to perish came upon him, and he caused the widow's heart to sing for joy."[256]

The memory of the just man shall be blessed.[257]

The second obituary appeared in *Poulson's American Daily Advertiser* on Friday, August 20, 1819. Again written by Major Jackson, it is a longer and more encompassing version of the first. The original copy found among the family papers includes an additional note in Jackson's handwriting that does not appear to be published elsewhere, "Thus go the relicks [sic] of a great mind." This second obituary reads:

DIED, on the 16th instant, after a long illness, which he bore with exemplary fortitude, in the 69th year of his age, WILLIAM LEWIS, Esquire, Senior Counsellor of the Pennsylvania Bar.

Obeying the strong influence of his genius, Mr. Lewis, at an early age exchanged the pursuits of Agriculture for the study of the Law, and placing himself under the instruction of the late Nicholas Waln, Esquire, whose confidence and esteem he acquired while his Pupil, he succeeded to his business and practice—and, uniting laborious diligence with extreme aptitude, he soon attained an eminence in his profession, which, during a course of forty years he supported with the most splendid success.

On the organization of the present government of the United States, Mr. Lewis was appointed District Attorney for Pennsylvania, and, on the death of the late Judge Hopkinson, President WASHINGTON, without solicitation conferred upon him the office of District Judge. In deference to the appointment, Mr. Lewis administered its duties for a short time, but as it did not comport with his private arrangements, he resigned, and returned to the Bar, where he continued, with his accustomed distinction, until declining health compelled him to seek repose on his farm, where he died.

Occasionally called to the councils of the Commonwealth, as a member of the State Legislature and Convention—the duties of those important stations were discharged with his exertions, in a peculiar degree, is the State of Pennsylvania indebted for the independence of the Judiciary.

The friend of freedom, he took a decided interest in the abolition of personal slavery, and the grateful expression of the emancipated sons of Africa, in their attendance at his funeral, attested their high sense of the obligations, which, as their Advocate, he had conferred upon them.

Benevolent in his disposition, he was warm and faithful in his friendship—and he extended his beneficence wherever the opportunity and means were in his power.

Respected and regretted by those to whom he was intimately known, he left an impression of his worth which will be long and affectionately cherished.[258]

Major Jackson's obituary is indeed a fitting tribute to Lewis, especially from a man who knew him so intimately.

Epilogue:

1. Settling the Lewis Estate

The executors of Lewis's estate—his second wife Frances, his son Josiah, and his close friend William Rawle—would start work settling the estate with the publication of the following in Poulson's American Daily Advertiser on August 31, 1819:

> All Persons Indebted to the Estate of WILLIAM LEWIS, Esquire, deceased, are requested: to whom all persons having demand on the same estate are desired to tender their account.[259]

While Lewis's wife Frances would enjoy the annual interest and income arising from one-third of Lewis's lands and tenements, plus any monies due to Lewis at the time of his death, the rest of Lewis's estate was divided as follows:

Josiah (son): three-ninths
Margaret (daughter): two-ninths
Louisa (granddaughter): two-ninths
Lewis Conover (grandson and son of deceased daughter Martha): two-ninths

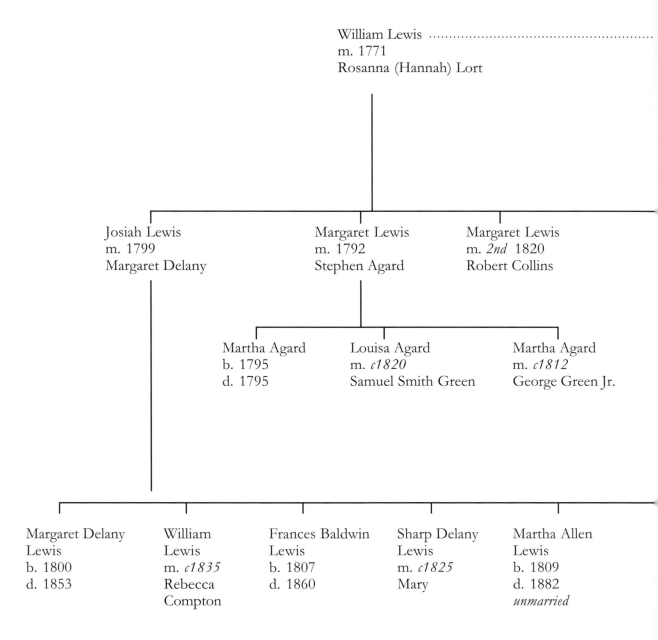

William Lewis ···
m. 1771
Rosanna (Hannah) Lort

Josiah Lewis
m. 1799
Margaret Delany

Margaret Lewis
m. 1792
Stephen Agard

Margaret Lewis
m. *2nd* 1820
Robert Collins

Martha Agard
b. 1795
d. 1795

Louisa Agard
m. *c1820*
Samuel Smith Green

Martha Agard
m. *c1812*
George Green Jr.

Margaret Delany
Lewis
b. 1800
d. 1853

William
Lewis
m. *c1835*
Rebecca
Compton

Frances Baldwin
Lewis
b. 1807
d. 1860

Sharp Delany
Lewis
m. *c1825*
Mary

Martha Allen
Lewis
b. 1809
d. 1882
unmarried

William Lewis
m. *2nd* 1801
Frances Esmonde Durdin
widow of Richard Durdin

Martha Lewis
m. 1795
Samuel Conover

Maria Fisher
*granddaughter of
Frances Durdin*

Lewis Henry Conover
m.
Elizabeth K. Sloan

Josiah Lewis
b. 1811
d. 1815

Mary Ann Delany
Lewis
m. 1831
Joseph Wragg

Josiah Lewis
m. *c1845*
Arabella Cahoon

Samuel Allen
Lewis

Phebe E. Lewis
b. 1820

Thomas R.D.
Lewis
b. 1822

Credit Sandra Hewlett, Certified Genealogist

Of all his family, Lewis seemed most concerned for the welfare of his daughter Margaret Agard and her daughter Louisa Agard, who were both unmarried at the time of his death. He makes no mention of Louisa's sister, Martha, presumably removed from the will because of her marriage to George Green, Jr. None of son Josiah's eight surviving children are mentioned, but perhaps the great number of his offspring accounts for why he garnered an extra ninth of the estate. Josiah and his wife, Margaret Delany Lewis, would have two more children after Lewis's death.

Soon after her father's death, Margaret Agard would marry Robert Collins of Montgomery County. Collins was an administrator who worked in Lewis's law office. The new Mrs. Collins would later, in 1832, deed a majority of her shares of the estate to her daughter Martha Green. [260] Following her mother's example, Louisa Agard would finally marry her brother-in-law's cousin Samuel Green in 1820, whom she'd met several years earlier.

Lewis's wife Frances would leave Summerville and Philadelphia altogether, choosing to return to Sunbury, Pennsylvania, in Northumberland County, to a property she had received from her first husband's estate. Frances's granddaughter resided in that area, and her stepson, Josiah, and his family lived not too far up the Susquehanna River in Wilkes-Barre. Two months after her husband's death, Frances and Rawle—as executors of the estate—leased the Summerville property to John Page. This arrangement lasted until the property was sold off by the sheriff of Philadelphia.

The events surrounding how and why the sheriff ended up selling Summerville—the house and the property in its entirety—are largely unknown. There is some knowledge that Lewis's estate took a large financial hit as a result of some land speculation. Lewis, like many of his contemporaries, owned a good deal of land. Although considered a small landowner compared to the likes of Robert Morris and William Bingham, he had at one point owned much of the undeveloped land in what is now South Philadelphia. Beyond investments in city lots, in the 1780s Lewis apparently began speculating in western Pennsylvania lands and later in Kentucky.[261] The exact number of acres held by the Lewis family has never been determined, but family correspondence makes reference to several different plots of land with varying acreage: Sandy River in Carter County, Clearfield in Rowan County, Blue Lick land in Nicholas County, ten thousand acres in Bourbon County and, as late as 1847, a reference to 6,800 acres in Hardin County. This sort of land speculation bankrupted a number of high-profile individuals during this time period, including Robert Morris. How profound the loss was to the Lewis estate is unknown. But these particular issues prevented Lewis's estate from being settled for a good number of years.

Early on, both Frances and Josiah discontinued their positions as executors, leaving William Rawle as the sole acting executor. Rawle hired a Kentucky lawyer to help recover the properties in question—as was outlined in an agreement dated October 8, 1821, involving a Mr. Wickcliffe, Esq.—which allowed Wickcliffe access to one half of the lands recovered as compensation for his services in relation to them. [262]

An auditor's report on the estate, filed with the Orphans Court of Philadelphia County on July 16, 1835, sheds further light on the activities of William Rawle:

> by the will of Mr. Lewis his executors are constituted general trustees and stewards of his real estate, with most extensive powers and authorities in relation to the recovery, superintendence, management and sale of the same. The Kentucky lands were involved in lawsuits and difficulties, and the services of Mr. Rawle, who was the only acting executor, appear to have been constantly in requisition for many years and to have been

of a very troublesome and laborious character. A vast amount of documentary evidence in support of the charge was laid before your auditor, including the correspondence of Mr. Rawle with Mr. Wickcliffe and others in relation to the business. Your auditor had not gone half through the evidence before he was entirely satisfied that the executor had faithfully earned all he had demanded, and that if a heavier charge had been made, it would have been much easier to sustain than defeat it.[263]

How could these Kentucky lands cause so much turmoil? The state of Kentucky, first formed in 1792, was actually land administered by the Commonwealth of Virginia. The area quickly gained a reputation for its rich soil and promises of unlimited resources and opportunity for wealth, thanks to a plethora of propaganda distributed by the original land speculators and accounts of travelers and settlers published in newspapers. Virginia's lack of efficiency and complexity in its Kentucky land policy in the late 1770s resulted in a great number of disputed land claims even when investors believed they actually held the proper land warrants. The land was overpromised, especially when Virginia officials promised lands in payment of services rendered to its soldiers during the Revolutionary War. Even further, some settlers just moved onto lands and laid claim. Even after the Lewis estate was settled, Lewis's heirs were still dealing with the vagaries of this land speculation. Correspondence between Sharp Lewis, Lewis's grandson, and the Kentucky lawyer Robert Wickcliffe continued up through 1857.

As time progressed, the Lewis family dynamic continued to change. Granddaughter Louisa Agard Green would die in May of 1827, leaving her husband, Samuel Green, as the beneficiary of her shares of the estate. The 1835 auditor's report noted that Green was advanced nine dollars on May 11, 1827, for a "coffin for Mrs. Green."[264] Grandson Lewis Conover died in May of 1828. He was survived by his wife, Elizabeth K. Sloan. Lewis's second wife, Frances Durdin Lewis, died in October of 1834. Her portion of the estate would go to her granddaughter from her first marriage, Maria Fisher.

By this time, William Rawle's son, William Jr., would continue to represent the interests of Josiah, Margaret Agard, and the administrators of the Conover estate, while the interests of Louisa Agard were represented by her husband, Samuel Green, and his own lawyer.

The estate was finally settled on July 15, 1835, sixteen years after Lewis's death.

Lewis's daughter Margaret Agard Collins would die in September of 1838 of gastritis at the age of sixty-five and was buried in the Friends cemetery. Her funeral expenses of $12.12 were paid by Hannah Jones, who is believed to be her cousin through Margaret's grandmother Barbara Jones.[265] Margaret's daughter, Martha Agard Green, enjoyed a long life. Although her husband, George Green, died in 1843, she would live for eighty-four years, dying in December 1882.

At some point, presumably after his father's death, son Josiah moved his large family to the area of Wilkes-Barre, in Luzerne County, Pennsylvania. Josiah and Margaret added two more children to their brood, a daughter in 1820 and a son in 1822. Josiah kept up a friendship and correspondence with William Rawle after he left Philadelphia. A letter to Rawle, dated September 29, 1821, documents some physical injuries that Josiah described as "lameness."[266] Similar correspondence showed that by 1824 he had suffered a second accident, and a third mishap in 1837 left Josiah physically impaired for the balance of his life. He would live until 1851. Several of Josiah's sons followed in their grandfather's footsteps. Grandson William Lewis would, like his namesake, become a successful attorney and lived until 1889. Grandson Sharp Lewis would take the lead on administering the Kentucky lands and other holdings on behalf of the family.

2. The Land Title History of Summerville

In August of 1783, William Lewis purchased thirteen acres, three roods, and eight perches of land—including use of a thirty-two foot lane—just north of downtown Philadelphia for £1,700 gold and silver Pennsylvania money.[267] This tract of land (later referred to as "lot A") had been part of the Hood family's Northern Liberties holdings and today is part of Fairmount Park. Although quite rural at the time, the land was adjacent to the Ridge Road (modern-day Ridge Avenue), which was an important route in and out of Philadelphia. To the north of the property was the Hood Tavern, and across the Ridge Road was Hoodbury, the Hood family estate that occupied much of what is presently considered the Strawberry Mansion neighborhood. Much of the land on the west side of Ridge Road (present-day wooded parkland) was under cultivation as pasture and gardens serving

Contemporary photo of Historic Strawberry Mansion. Photo by Fred Pfaff.

the Philadelphia market. Lewis's land purchase included a stone farmhouse built by William Coxe, who had held the land from 1757 to 1770.

His property was contained in an area originally known to the Lenape Indians as Netopcom. The first European owners were the Swanson brothers, who had been given six hundred acres through a deed from William Penn. One of the brothers, Swan Swanson, sold his share—two hundred acres—to John Hood. In 1708, when Hood conveyed the land to his son, Thomas, the deed described:

> Buildings, houses, barns, outhouses, orchards, gardens, fields, fences, woods, underwoods, timber and trees, ways, waters, meadows, marshes with fishing, fowling & hunting with all other & all manner the appurtenances whatsoever thereunto belonging or in any wise appertaining.

Eventually, the grandson Thomas Jr. would receive approximately forty acres, and by 1757, he would sell approximately thirteen of those acres to William Coxe, who would then sell the same to Joseph Swift in 1770, with Lewis taking possession in August of 1783 of "all that Messuage, Plantation and Tract of Land."

In January of 1792, Lewis acquired an additional thirteen-and-a-half acres and twenty perches (referred to as "plot B" in legal documents) for £425 lawful money of Pennsylvania. Purchased from John Donaldson and his wife Sarah, this additional property contained a small house, a blacksmith's shop on the Wissahickon River, and another small house and fishery on the Schuylkill River. This second purchase of land was not recorded in the city deed book until the May 24, 1800, as it appears that Donaldson did not have clear title to the property at the time of purchase.

Two documents help provide the details of how Lewis developed the property during his time at Summerville: a rental agreement with John Page in October of 1819, just after Lewis's death, and the deed of purchase with Joseph Hemphill in 1821. These two documents list the following being contained on the property:

A capital stone messuage (also referred to as the Mansion House)
A stone kitchen adjoining thereto, and adjoining offices
A tenant's house of stone
A good coach house
A floored stable, with room for four horses and one cow
Barns and other stables
Milk house
Smoke house
Ice House along the Schuylkill
Fishery along Schuylkill
Two pumps of water
A quarry of excellent building stone convenient for water carriage (a causeway laid out along the side of the hill down to the river)
A number of good fruit trees

The papers note, additionally, that "the grounds are in a state of High Cultivation and Command an Extensive and Beautiful Prospect."

The rental agreement of 1819 illustrates that Summerville was indeed in high cultivation. It stipulated that:

> He [John Page] is to put the fields now in potatoes and turnips and also the orchard lot and the Robinhood lot into Winter Barley on shares. . . . He is to keep the fences and other parts of the place from damage by trespassers and others—the front and back lawns are not to be pastured (mowed) nor turned up nor is any wood to be cut. He is to be at liberty to fill the icehouse and to sell the contents for his own profit. What manure there is in or about the barns is to spread as a top dressing on the lawn—no manure or straw to be hauled away. He is to put the garden in order.

It was Summerville's second owner, Joseph Hemphill, who would add the two large wings to Lewis's original design, creating the exterior of the house as we recognize it today. Hemphill took ownership of the property in July of 1821, after the Lewis's estate was forced to sell. Hemphill's wife Margaret was the daughter of wealthy iron baron Robert Coleman. Despite his father-in-law's wealth, Hemphill would mortgage the property in 1838 to Harriet Coleman, a relative of his wife. As the mortgage was not repaid according to their agreement, Coleman filed suit against Hemphill and eventually gained control of the property shortly after Hemphill died in May of 1842. Apparently not having much interest in the property, Coleman attempted to dispose of it on several occasions, eventually selling to George Crock in 1846. Crock would farm the property for more than twenty years, after which he would sell the land to the city of Philadelphia in 1867.

BRIEF OF TITLE FOR SUMMERVILLE (STRAWBERRY MANSION)

Date	From	To	Description	Acknowledged	Deed Info
June 3, 1683	William Penn Proprietor and Governor in Chief of the Province of Pennsylvania	Swan Swanson, Woolly Swanson and Andrew Swanson, jointly	600 acres of land along the Schuykill at Netopcom in exchange for land in the Northern Liberties in the County of Philadelphia (present day Center City Philadelphia)	n/a	Deed no. 3
May 6, 1696	Swan, Woolly, and Andrew Swanson	Swan Swanson (200 acres)	Swan Swanson with others, partitioned said 600 acres, whereby there was allotted to said Swan Swanson 200 acres	n/a	Deed no.3
July 22, 1696	Swan Swanson	John Hood	in fee for said 200 acres of land under yearly quit rent	August 4, 1696	Recorded August 29, 1696 in Deed Book E2, vol 5, p 334
October 16, 1708	John Hood	Thomas Hood	in fee for said 200 acres of land yielding and paying the yearly quit rent of one half bushel of wheat to the hundred acres	April 6, 1756	Recorded April 17, 1756 in Deed Book H, no. 7, p 119
See also: 1719, 23 October... will of said John Hood giving to his son said Thomas Hood his heirs and assigns the land he bought of Swan Swanson. Proved 30 Sept 1721, registered in book of Wills D, p 197					
April 14, 1756	Thomas Hood Sr.	Thomas Hood Jr.	in fee for a tract of 40 3/4 acres (part of said 200 acres)	April 19, 1756	Book H, no 7, p 139
June 15, 1757	Thomas Hood Jr. and his wife Rebecca	William Coxe	in fee for a parcel of land containing 13 acres (part of said tract of 40 3/4 acres)	July 2, 1757	Book X, Vol 3, p 146
July 12, 1758	Thomas Hood Jr. and Rebecca	William Coxe his heirs	use, liberty and privilege of a 32 foot lane beginning at Wissahicken Road allowing ingress, egress an regress through Thomas Hood's land	March 7, 1763	By Rebecca (widow of Thomas Hood, Jr.)
May 29, 1770	William Coxe & wife Mary	Joseph Swift	messuage & tract of 13 acres, 3 roods and 8 perches of land and 32 foot lane	May 29, 1770	n/a
August 8, 1783	Joseph Swift & wife	William Lewis	in fee (1700£ gold & silver money of Pennsylvania) for same premises as above, later referred to as "lot A"	October 23, 1783	Deed book 12, p 435

BRIEF OF TITLE FOR SUMMERVILLE (STRAWBERRY MANSION)

Date	From	To	Description	Acknowledged	Deed Info
May 24, 1800	John Donaldson & wife Sarah	William Lewis	for fee in said track of 13 1/2 acres and 2 perches, later referred to as "lot B"	July 28, 1800	Deed Book EF, no.3, p 418 (deed #18)

July 1800, Lewis joins together lot A & lot B as recorded in deed book EF, no. 3, p 418–deed #18

June 1820, Frances Lewis, Josiah & William Rawle are appointed Executors of the Will of William Lewis as dated August 5, 1819 and registered in the book of Wills 7, p 46

June 1821, the Lewis Estate is sued by the Estate of George Taylor, deceased in absentia for a past debt which was levied & condemned to a value of $8000, forcing the sale of the Summerville

Date	From	To	Description	Acknowledged	Deed Info
July 21, 1821	Caleb North esq, High Sheriff of the City and County of PA	Joseph Hemphill	Lots A & B-totalling 27 acres, 63 perches for $10,600	Sept 17, 1821	Book C, p.320, Deed Book (GS), no 14, p259
July 11, 1837	Joseph Hemphill	Harriet Coleman	Mortgaged estate for $10,000	July 12, 1837	Mortgage Book LHF, no 6, p 486
June 18, 1842	High Sheriff of the City and County of PA	Harriet Coleman	Hemphill estate sold for $5000 after Coleman files suit against Hemphill in March 1842 for $11,300 which did not settle before Hemphill's death in May 1842	June 18, 1842 in Open District Court	Book M, p 116
October 1, 1846	Harriet Coleman	George Crock	Coleman had offered the grounds for sale as early as 1844	November 3, 1846	Deed Book A.W.M., no 21, p 79
November 6, 1867	George Crock	City of Philadelphia	Acknowledged by Eli K. Price, Chair of the Committee on Land Purchase, April 12, 1871	November 6, 1867	Deed Book (L.L.O.), no 98, p 142

Philadelphia City Archives "Title Papers, Fairmount Park Property" Box 3A, "George Crock, grantor" file

3. Summerville Becomes Historic Strawberry Mansion

Present day visitors to William Lewis's country villa often inquire as to how Summerville become known as Historic Strawberry Mansion—and its relation to the surrounding neighborhood that is also referred to by the same name. Such a simple question should have a simple answer, but this is not the case. Years of speculation and storytelling have created a number of incorrect theories that somehow found their way into the Philadelphia consciousness as fact. It wasn't until 1976, in fact, that an accurate answer would start to emerge. It was the time of the Bicentennial Celebration, and all the local Philadelphia institutions mounted celebratory exhibitions, bringing out long-buried treasures that had not been on display for countless years. Among these displays was a fine exhibit by the Historical Society of Pennsylvania featuring a large, rarely-viewed 1808 map of Philadelphia by John Hill. It was a revelation to find William Lewis's name listed as a property owner of "Summer Ville" on the banks of the Schuylkill River in an area listed as "Strawberry Hill." This mention of "Summer Ville" matched references located during that same period in family records, indicating that Lewis had indeed called his country villa Summerville.

Hill's map showed that Lewis never called his home Strawberry Mansion, but that Summerville

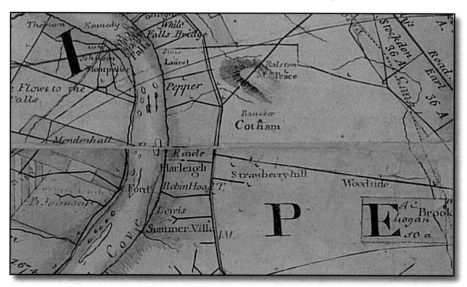

Section of John Hills's Map or Plan of the City of Philadelphia and Environs (1808) displaying "Lewis," "Summer Ville," and "Strawberry Hill." Historical Society of Pennsylvania.

was located in a section referred to as Strawberry Hill. Further research proved that "strawberry" was quite a popular name in the early nineteenth century. The father of the American navy, Commodore John Barry, named his country home, nearby on Frankford Avenue, Strawberry Hill. Several other properties in and around Philadelphia, into New Jersey, and beyond were also named Strawberry Hill.

Beyond the name, the fruit itself was also quite popular, as it was prevalent in both cultivated and wild forms throughout the city. There is evidence that strawberries were a favorite throughout the nascent nation, as illustrated by this extract from a Vermont newspaper in 1807:

> It is a fact, but not generally known, that the common Strawberry now in season, is a natural dentifrice; and that its juice, without any previous preparation whatever, dissolves the tartareous [sic] encrustations on the teeth, and makes the breath sweet and agreeable.

Hill's description of the area around Lewis's country home as "Strawberry Hill" seems logical based on advertisements of the time. In *Poulson's American Daily Advertiser* of June 21, 1810, a Mr. F. Montmollin posted the sale of property "just south of Robin Hood Tavern near the Wissahiccon [sic] road along the Schuylkill." The description included details of approximately 17 acres "in a high state of cultivation," along with an apple orchard and various other fruit trees, a two-acre garden, and a half acre of strawberries. Similarly, the paper on April 15, 1813, listed a similar property on Hart's Lane, just above Robin Hood Tavern, which boasted the "best of Fruit, and Flower Gardens, with abundance of Straw-berries, Rass-berries, [and] Currants."[268]

Other advertisements indicate that the area attracted city dwellers for relaxation and refreshments. On January 24, 1774, a Mr. C. Cooper placed an announcement in the *Pennsylvania Packet* to inform "the public in general, and his friends in particular, that he hath removed from Philadelphia to the tavern known by the name Robin Hood, on the Ridge Road, near the Falls of Schuylkill and four miles from the city, where he proposes to keep the best entertainment for man and horse, he hopes to meet with encouragement."[269]

As the cultivation of strawberries increased, so too did the public's demand for them—especially strawberries with cream and what became known as "iced cream." Though it was not invented here, Philadelphians developed quite a strong reputation for ice cream by the end of the eighteenth century. When the city became the seat of government and George Washington was the first President; "iced creams" were often served at the presidential Thursday dinners. Those lucky enough to possess fruit trees and gardens as well as a milk cow often invited the public to come and partake of this delicacy. "Strawberry-gardens," as they became known, "offered their heated and thirsty visitors some cooling delicious fruit bathed in rich, fresh cream." In June 1808, notice was given that Strawberry Hill, beyond the Robin Hood Tavern on Ridge road, was open for the reception of company, as "it was provided with an abundance of excellent strawberries and cream."[270] In this case, the Strawberry Hill referenced is likely the area referenced on Hill's map.

Information about these strawberry gardens as reported in the 1884 edition of Scharf and Westcott's *History of Philadelphia* might have given rise to the notion that strawberries were served directly from the porch of Historic Strawberry Mansion in the Hemphill days, as was originally presented by the Committee of 1926 when they first opened the house to visitors.[271] Others believe that Joseph Hemphill renamed the house in the early 1830s after he added the Greek Revival wings to William Lewis's federal-style home. Paint analysis uncovered pink paint dating back to this period, leaving some to wonder whether the name influenced the color choice or vice versa.[272] It is more likely that a strawberry garden (or several) was merely located adjacent to the villa. It does not, however, seem an overstatement to suggest that the area colloquially referenced as "Strawberry Hill" soon encompassed a larger area than Hill's 1808 map portrayed—eventually extending to the river to include Summerville and Robin Hood Tavern and beyond.

It is more difficult to determine exactly when the area of Strawberry Hill became known as *Strawberry Mansion*. In 1842, the same year Harriet Coleman took possession of the property, Augustus Kollner painted a watercolor of the house and entitled the work Strawberry Mansion. Interestingly, written in pencil beneath the title is the inscription "strawberry house." A print of this Kollner watercolor is part of the permanent collection of Historic Strawberry Mansion; it was presented to the Committee of 1926 by Fitz Eugene Dixon in 1989 in honor of the mansion's 200th anniversary. Yet another example of the change in name comes from an advertisement in 1848:

> Learnor Assembly of Spring Garden—second annual picnic party—To be given at Strawberry Manssion *[sic]*, On Monday, the (4th) of July. To start from the Native American Hall, on the Ridge Road, at (?) o'clock—posted by J. W. Trout, Secretary.[273]

Evidently the terms "strawberry hill" and "strawberry mansion" were used interchangeably throughout the next twenty years or so. An 1869 report published by the Philadelphia Water Department references a particular reservoir as being "on Strawberry Mansion property."[274] But several years later, in 1875, when the Fairmount Park Commission converted the villa into a restaurant, they named it Strawberry Hill, not Strawberry Mansion. The property, originally purchased by the City of Philadelphia in 1867, had become the site of an important steamboat landing.[275] With its magnificent view of the Schuylkill River and the surrounding area, it soon became a popular restaurant featuring strawberries and cream on the menu. This fact led some to believe that the restaurant was the genesis of the Strawberry Mansion name, but as we see, the reference existed before the restaurant did. Additionally, we find that contemporary references to the restaurant use the name Strawberry Hill, as Sarah B. Wister did when she wrote to her son Owen (author of *The Virginian*) in a letter dated October 2, 1875:

> On Tuesday Mr. Henry James came in for a couple of days to say good bye before sailing for Europe, which he does this month. As I was cookless we drove to the park and dined at Strawberry Hill on the Piazza & it was perfectly beautiful, day and all.[276]

Vintage 1898 Strawberry Mansion postcard. From the author's collection.

Vintage Strawberry Mansion postcard (date unknown). From the author's collection.

Evidently the neighborhood influenced the menu rather than the menu influencing the naming of the neighborhood, as has been erroneously reported through the years. Yet by the time the Committee of 1926 opened the house to visitors, the name Strawberry Hill seems to have lost favor, and Strawberry Mansion became the preference. Referencing the house as Historic Strawberry Mansion was useful in helping to differentiate the building from the Strawberry Mansion neighborhood that surrounded it.

Just as important, Hill's 1808 map helped clear up another misconception about the history of Strawberry Mansion. The original belief was that William Lewis's Summerville had actually been called Somerton. Early interpretive materials published by the Pennsylvania Museum of Art (present-day Philadelphia Museum of Art) reported that the original farmhouse on Lewis's property had been owned and occupied by Charles Thomson, the Secretary of the Continental Congress, and that it had been burned to the ground in 1777 by British troops.[277] Hill's map shows two properties: Summerville and another two-hundred-acre property on nearby Germantown Road owned by the prominent Norris family, called Somerville (and often referred to as Somerton). It was the Norrises' Somerville house that was destroyed by fire. Believing Charles Thomson was residing on the premises with his wife Hannah Harrison, granddaughter of merchant Isaac Norris, the British came looking for official documents of the Continental Congress they assumed would be in the care of the secretary. The close proximity of the two houses, along with their similar names, Summerville and Somerville, led to a good bit of the confusion in later years. Further still, the 1941 publication of the popular book "Strawberry Mansion: First Known as Somerton, the House of Many Masters," by Sarah Dickson Lowrie, helped propagate these misconceptions.

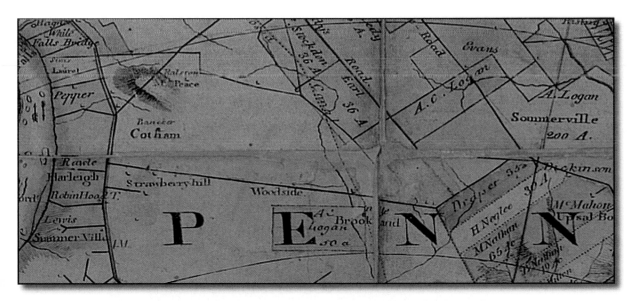

Section of John Hills's 1808 map, illustrating relation of "Summer Ville", on left, to "Somerville," on right. Historical Society of Pennsylvania.

Today Historic Strawberry Mansion is governed by the Fairmount Park Commission of the Philadelphia Parks and Recreation Department and is still administered by the Committee of 1926.

Historic Strawberry Mansion is the largest of the eight noteworthy Fairmount Park Houses, which are considered to be among the most significant architectural examples of eighteenth- and early nineteenth-century homes in the United States. Open to the public for tours throughout the year, Historic Strawberry Mansion features a stellar collection of period furnishings and artifacts focused on the residence of its first two owners, William Lewis and Joseph Hemphill. Further information about the house can be found at www.historicstrawberrymansion.org.

As the name Strawberry Hill faded from use the area surrounding Lewis's Summerville changed from agriculture to the heart of Fairmount Park's more than nine thousand acres—a well-used and well-loved urban oasis. The house itself would become the epicenter of what would later be regarded as the Strawberry Mansion neighborhood. If some of those older names had not been lost through time and change, how lovely it would be if perhaps today William Lewis's country home was known as Summerville on Strawberry Hill.

Contemporary postcard of Historic Strawberry Mansion. From the author's collection.

Contemporary postcard featuring the William Lewis room at Historic Strawberry Mansion (note the circa 1950s copy of the Gilbert Stuart portrait by Nicholas Cortiglia). From the author's collection.

Committee of 1926, staff, and McFarland family. From left to right: Melissa Trotter Horvat, Anthony Horvat, Beth Kowalchick, Kathybeth Jerome, Sean Nally, George C. McFarland, Jr., George C. McFarland III, Esther Ann McFarland. Photo by Alan Kolc for the 2012 Academy Ball program.

Appendix I

The Swedish Settlements (and their connections to William Lewis and Historic Strawberry Mansion)

On the south side of Philadelphia's majestic City Hall there exists a little-noticed bronze tablet with the inscription, "In Commemoration of the Swedish Settlements on the Delaware, 1639–1655." The fact that Philadelphia and parts of Pennsylvania, before they were so named, were settled by Swedish colonists is an often-forgotten fact, eclipsed by the later arrival of William Penn. One might say the Swedes are overshadowed by Penn just as that small bronze commemoration plaque is overshadowed by the larger-than-life Calder statue of Penn atop City Hall. Most citizens of Philadelphia, and even many visitors, are aware of Penn's presence overhead and the story of his Philadelphia landing. How many thousands of people walk by the tablet each day unaware of its existence and the early adventures of the Swedes?

William Lewis would have been aware of the journey of the Swedish colonists as his first wife, Rosanna Lort, was descended from the original settlers of the area. Rosanna's great-grandmother Gertrude had arrived in New Sweden (present-day Delaware) in 1640 with her father, Sven Gunnarsson, and other family members. Gertrude's brothers Swan, Andrew, and Woolley Swanson (anglicized from Sven, Anders, and Olave Svensson) would gain significant land ownership in the new colony. Gertrude would marry Jonas Nilsson, a soldier who had accompanied the third royal governor to the colony in 1643 to guard Fort Christina. The family's roots grew deep in the forty years between their arrival and William Penn's.

It was, however, not just Lewis's wife and children who brought Swedish roots to his country villa. The land on which Summerville stood had the same Swedish roots as those of his family, as the first owner of the land on which the house stood was none other than Rosanna's great-uncle Swan Swanson. How Swan Swanson came into possession of the Netopcom land—and its relation to William Penn's plans for building his dream city—is a little-known story in Philadelphia history.

The Swedes, following the English in Virginia (1607), the Dutch in New York (1614), and a second group of English in Massachusetts (Plymouth 1620), became the fourth settlement in the New World when they settled in Delaware in 1638.[278] That year the ships *Kalmar Nyckel* and *Fogel Grip* arrived at the Rocks on the Delaware River with enough provisions and manpower to build Fort Christina at present day Wilmington. Twenty-four men were left to guard the fort—the start of New Sweden. In 1640 the *Kalmar Nyckel* returned, bringing the first families to New Sweden (including Sven Gunnarsson and his family), and then returned once more in 1641 bearing another large group. By 1643, when Queen Christina's new governor, Colonel Johan Printz, was dispatched to take over New Sweden, the residents had settled on lands bordering both sides of the Delaware River—into present-day Delaware and South Jersey. Governor Printz arrived along with fifty new settlers (including soldier Jonas Nilsson) on the ships *Fama* and *Swan*.

Upon Printz's arrival at Fort Christina, however, he found that its location did not abide by the specific instructions he had received before he left Stockholm, which indicated the need to build a fort that would strengthen Sweden's control of the region.[279] The success of New Sweden depended upon it. Sailing up river from Fort Christina, Printz chose a location named Tinicum Island (in present-day Pennsylvania) because it offered a strategic location on the west side of the Delaware River, just south of the Schuylkill River. On this island, the fort would dominate both rivers and control the valuable fur trade. He immediately ordered construction of a massive new fort named New Göttenburg, including a trading post and a personal residence—a "very handsome" mansion called Printzhof. New Göttenburg would become the first permanent European settlement in Pennsylvania, founded one year before William Penn was born and thirty-nine years before his arrival in the New World.[280]

In March 1644, when construction of the fort was nearly complete, New Göttenburg replaced Fort Christina as the capital of New Sweden, and the Swedish government deeded Tinicum Island to the governor and his heirs. Unfortunately, on November 25, 1645, Printz's grand home with imported Swedish details burned to the ground along with most of the buildings inside the fort complex. Despite his poor luck on Tinicum Island, the governor had a job to do, and his instructions from Stockholm were both specific and deliberate. Article 5 of these instructions, dated August 15, 1642, charged him to "extend, in virtue of the articles of the contract entered into with the wild inhabitants of the country, as its rightful lords." Article 9 decreed:

> The wild nations, bordering on all sides, the Governor shall treat with all humanity and respect, and so that no violence or wrong be done to them by Her Royal Majesty [Queen Christina] or Her subjects aforesaid; but he shall rather . . . exert himself that the same wild people may be gradually instructed in the truths and worship of the

Christian religion, and in other ways brought to civilization and good government, and in this manner properly guided. Especially shall he seek to gain their confidence, and impress upon their minds that neither he, the Governor, nor his people and subordinates are come into these parts to do them any wrong, or injury, but much more for the purpose of furnishing them with such things as they may need for the ordinary wants of life.[281]

Simply put, the Swedes did not envision themselves conquerors but, rather, evangelicals tasked with converting the natives to Christianity while simultaneously teaching them proper (Swedish) culture and government. The principals of peace and respect were of utmost important to the Swedes. Dr. William M. Reynolds, in the introduction to his translation of Acreliius's *History of New Sweden*, emphasizes that it was actually the Swedes who inaugurated the peaceful policy carried out by William Penn in their purchase of lands from the Lenape and in their friendly manner with them. The Swedes were confident enough in their relations with the Lenape as to mingle freely among them. It is said that not one Swede was harmed from any Indian from whom they had purchased their lands. Of how successful they were in their evangelical pursuits we have less knowledge. The Reverend John Campanius made the first translation of the Lutheran catechism into the idiom of the Lenni Lenape dialect and even adapted them to their circumstances. In this manner, "give us this day our daily bread" became "give us this day a plentiful supply of venison and corn."[282]

Like the earlier European settlements, New Sweden was fraught with many difficulties. Intermittent support from the homeland was a continual issue as Queen Christina battled for control of other areas back home. Lack of food was also problematic, while the pressure to maintain control of the region remained constant and paramount. The Dutch provided steady pressure in their labors to gain control of the Delaware River and access to the fur trades. Governor Printz was also forced to handle criticism from his own Swedish settlers who were unhappy with his administrative capabilities. The early Swedish settlers expected "to partake in the administration of their local, secular, and religious affairs," as they had learned from the self-government of their home country.[283] Issues involving decisions made by Printz in both 1652 and 1653 resulted in a formal complaint. Filed and signed by twenty-two men (including Sven Gunnarsson), it accused the governor of autocratic rule. The governor branded the petition a mutiny and accused several men, including one of his own soldiers, of instigation. After Governor Printz had his soldier killed by a firing squad, he returned to Sweden in haste.[284] New Sweden was left in disarray with Johan Papegoja, the governor's son-in-law, left in charge. Several colonists decide to leave New Sweden, fleeing to the Dutch settlement at Fort Casimir and further south to a settlement in Maryland.

By the following year, 1654, the capital of New Sweden reverted back to Fort Christina and the colonial population had settled out to approximately seventy men, women, and children. The remaining settlers discussed whether it might be prudent to unite with the Dutch at Fort Casimir. The point was rendered moot as the ship *Orn* soon arrived in New Sweden with a new governor, Johan Rising, along with 250 passengers. Despite Printz's earlier arrangements with the Dutch, the new governor immediately captured Fort Casimir, renaming it Fort Trinity. The Swedes once again enjoyed total control of the Delaware River. At this point, many of the Dutch settlers decided to leave the area and headed north to New Amsterdam (present-day New York). Governor Rising helped to diffuse the internal wrath experienced by the former Governor by introducing reforms to insure property rights to freemen. Despite Governor Rising's improvements, the colony was still plagued by hunger and disease. In September of 1655, Dutch Governor Stuyvesant enacted revenge on the new Swedish governor and invaded New Sweden with seven armed ships and more than three hundred soldiers. With the total population of New Sweden less than the number of Dutch soldiers, the Swedes had no choice but to surrender without a fight. Governor Rising returned to Sweden accompanied by at least thirty-six other Swedes. The remaining settlers were asked to swear their allegiance to the Dutch.[285]

In the following year, fourteen more Swedes and ninety-two Finns arrived upon the ship *Mercurius* in the now Dutch-controlled colony. The Dutch initially blocked the *Mercurius* from sailing past Fort Casimir on its journey up the Delaware River. But the Indians—still friends of the Swedes—intervened by climbing aboard the ship and ushering it to directly to Tinicum Island. The Dutch were persuaded to allow the Swedes (along with their fellow Finnish colonists) the ability to self-govern in the area north of the Christina River. Further, the Dutch approved a Swedish-run court (Upland Court) and a militia. Meanwhile, the Dutch acquired additional land—New Amstel—south of the Christina River in present-day New Castle, Delaware. In 1663 the Dutch Governor Stuyvesant began to issue land patents to Swedish settlers.[286] The next year, control of the area north of the Christina River was transferred from Governor Stuyvesant to those in power at New Amstel. By this time, the Swedes (including Jonas Nilsson, and Sven Gunnarsson and his family) had moved into the areas of Passyunk, Wicaco, and Moyamensing (present-day Center City, West, and South Philadelphia). These Swedish families received property patents confirming their rights from D'Hinojossa, the head of New Amstel.[287] Property patents and maps of the Wicaco area issued during this time frame, and later recorded and honored by the English, referred to Sven's sons as "Swan Swanson and company."

Shortly thereafter, English warships arrived and seized the New Amstel colony from the Dutch. The Swedes and Finns were assured by the English that their property rights and freedoms would not be affected. Upland Court was allowed to self-govern as before. By the time the first English census of the region was taken in 1671, there were approximately 165 households between New Castle and Burlington Island (near present-day Burlington, New Jersey). Except for a few pockets of English, these census takers found the population to be overwhelmingly Swedish and Finnish. Throughout the rest of the decade, Upland Court continued to operate, increasing the number of justices to six. Additionally, the Swedes were granted permission to build a new log church at Wicaco on land donated by the Swanson brothers (the site of present-day Gloria Dei Church, or Old Swedes', on Columbus Avenue.) The new log church was dedicated in 1677, and Paster Jacobus Fabritius, a German from Manhattan, became the minister. By 1680 Upland Court integrated two English justices upon the retirement of two of the Swedes.[288]

The Swanson title or patent of Wicaco—which comprised roughly the area of Philadelphia one

Southeast view of the Old Swedes' Church, Southwark, watercolor by William L. Breton, 1828. Historical Society of Pennsylvania.

mile west of Delaware River, running from the proximity of present-day Vine Street to Washington Avenue—was first confirmed by Governor Lovelace on May 31, 1671, and was further confirmed by a survey made by Richard Noble on June 12, 1681, under the instruction of Upland Court.[289] This survey holds special interest in that it is one of the earliest land records in Philadelphia in which the boundaries are given in approximate measure. Though the measures were crudely described, they were thought to be quite accurate. The original of this survey resides in the Pennsylvania State Archives. It was at the southern tip of this land, adjacent to the Delaware River, that the new log church at Wicaco was built. One of the first roads featured in this survey, referenced as Wicaco Lane, was used by the settlers to travel to the Wicaco Church. Wicaco Lane, sometimes referred to as Lovers' Lane, was renamed Prime Street and today is known as Washington Avenue. By the early 1680s, the brothers Swanson, along with their fellow Swedes and Finns, a smattering of Dutch and English, and, of course, the Lenape Indians, had all settled into a relatively peaceful existence, unaware that big changes were coming their way.

In England, on March 4, 1681, King Charles II signed a charter making William Penn the world's largest sole, non-royal landowner by granting him over forty-five thousand square miles of land and sovereign rule of said territory with all rights and privileges except the power to declare war. The land consisted of territory south of New Jersey and north of Maryland (which belonged to Lord Baltimore). This charter meant that New Sweden was now under control of William Penn.

Penn quickly went to work. That same year he sent William Markham to the region to arrange a transition plan. Planning to build a model city at Upland (present-day Chester, Pennsylvania), he sent three commissioners to purchase the land and supervise settlement. When his team arrived at Upland in the fall of 1681, they found that the Swedish settlers were not willing to sell their property. The Swedes had lived there for decades. Buying them out was deemed expensive, and forcing them to vacate was seen as unchristian. Not wanting to alienate the affections of these particular Swedes, the commissioners continued upstream and came upon a location they thought might be advantageous. It was a large piece of land between the Schuylkill and Delaware Rivers, a largely undeveloped area on high ground known to the Lenape as Coaquannock —meaning pine grove— and known to the Swedes as the property of the three Swanson brothers (Swan, Woolley, and Andrew).

Much has been written about the arrival of William Penn in the fall of 1682. Penn's legacy is so strong that it has mostly obliterated the story of the settlers who came to the region before him. Many strong images, such as Benjamin West's 1772 painting depicting the Treaty of Friendship between Penn and Lenape Chief Tamanend, reinforce Penn's principles of fairness, peace, and social justice. Generations of Pennsylvanians have grown up believing that Penn negotiated with the chief to gain access to the land for his new city. On the occasion one actually finds mention of the Swedes in relation to this land, we are informed that the Swansons sold their land to Penn's commissioners well before Penn's arrival to the colony. The truth is that the transaction between Penn and the Swanson family, and indeed his transactions with many of the original settlers, was anything but simple. In order for Penn to build his dream city he would first have to convince the Swanson brothers to relinquish the land they had built their lives around, a strategically located plantation to which they had held English title for more than a decade prior to Penn's arrival and the Dutch title for the decade prior to the arrival of the English.

In the summer of 1682 Thomas Holme began to lay out Penn's "greene country towne" that incorporated the land owned by the Swanson brothers. Penn's vision was to create both a beautiful and healthful city in contrast to that of seventeenth-century London, which suffered plague, fire, and any number of catastrophes.[290] Holme laid out an orderly grid with large green spaces, as Penn believed that public parks and wide streets would be the key to keeping the citizens healthy and preventing the spread of fire. He named the streets that ran east and west after native trees and plants: Chestnut, Cranberry, Locust, Mulberry, Strawberry, Walnut, and Vine. So beautiful was this vision that Penn quickly put Holme's map, entitled *A Portrait of the City of Philadelphia*, and a later version detailing the progress of settlement and land ownership into promotional use in England. While Penn promoted his new colony back in Europe, his local agents continued pressing forward with his plans for the new city.

By 1683, the Swedes' Upland Court had been abolished and replaced with English courts in Philadelphia, Chester, and Bucks Counties. The Swedes and Finns were once again required to swear their allegiance, this time to the king of England. Penn leveraged the Swedes' relationship with the native Lenape Indians by hiring them to negotiate new and ongoing Indian treaties. Penn's promotions of his new colony, the "holy experiment" created to foster religious and political freedom, started to produce results. Twenty-three ships carrying hundreds of English Quaker settlers arrived in the colony, followed by ships from Wales, Germany, Holland, and other areas from which citizens hoped to escape religious persecution in this new land. The Swedes quickly found themselves outnumbered. Eventually, it seems the Swanson brothers were "convinced" to surrender approximately six hundred acres of their Wicaco plantation. Other Swedes gave up additional adjoining lands. All were promised compensating lands elsewhere. They would be leaving not just an advantageous location situated between two rivers for someplace yet to be determined, but they would be leaving their homes and place of worship. Even Penn's promise of more land could not make up those losses.

"Old Swede Loghouse, Christian Street, north side of Swanson Street", watercolor by David J. Kennedy, 1864. David J. Kennedy Watercolors, Historical Society of Pennsylvania.

The introductory portion of Penn's deed to the Swanson brothers reads:

WILLIAM PENN late Proprietor and Governor in Chief of the said Province, soon after he became Proprietor of the same and before the City of Philadelphia was seated therein, did grant unto Swan Swanson, Woolley Swanson, and Andrew Swanson in exchange for the land on which the City of Philadelphia is now laid out and seated, as by warrant under his Hand & Seal dated 3rd day of the 6th month 1683 to the SURVEYOR GENERAL for the laying out of the same and returned into the Proprieteries Secretaries' office.[291]

The land promised to the Swanson brothers in exchange for their Wacaco property was recorded as 820 acres west of the city, along the Schuylkill River in an area known to the Indians as Netopcom.[292] Ultimately the brothers were given only six hundred acres of land. No one can state for certain how the Swanson brothers or their neighbors felt about Penn's land exchange program. There are, however, several compelling sources that illuminate the topic. The Pennsylvania Archives highlights a particular occasion recorded by John Reed in 1774 which illustrates a great deal of dissatisfaction between "the people" and Penn's "commissioners of property":

> very great abuses have been and are put upon the inhabitants, and extortions used by the secretary, surveyors, and Other officers concerned in property as well as courts, which might have been prevented (or sooner remedied) had thou been pleased to pass the bill proposed by the Assembly, in the year 1701, to regulate fees; as also the want of a surveyor-general, which is a great injury and dissatisfaction to the people; as likewise the want of an established judicature for trials between thee and the people: for if we exhibit our complaints against thee, or those who represent thee instate or property, they must be determined by or before justices of they own appointment by which means, though become, in a legal sense, judge in thy own cause, &c.[293]

It was not just the original settlers who were suffering. The incoming colonists had their gripes as well. For example, the Welsh Quakers had come to Pennsylvania to create what they hoped would be a Welsh barony where their plantations would be laid out adjacent to each other so as to constitute one contiguous settlement.[294] The Welsh had even met with Penn in London in late 1681 to work out their plan. The typical sale of land was in lots of five thousand acres. Welsh patentees assigned each block of land to a "company," the whole of which consisted of seven companies. A trustee for each company then distributed the appropriate acres to each individual investor. This particular settlement never quite materialized, as the Welsh had been persuaded that a written contract was not necessary as long as they signed their names to the general Articles of Concession. The Welsh were also given Penn's personal promise to protect their interests. It appears that Penn made his promise in good faith, but large sums of money were at stake in all of the promises he made to all of the settlers. If the colony failed, he would have been ruined. Upon arrival, the Welsh found that purchasing the land from Penn in England was quite different from getting a "warrant of survey" (an oral request to locate on a particular piece of land) from Penn's agents once they arrived in Pennsylvania. It could take days to locate the agents, and once located, they were known to be susceptible to bribes and petty prejudices. The Welsh had relied on Penn, a fellow Quaker, and they were very disappointed. They reluctantly compromised and settled on lands on the west side of the Schuylkill River at present-day Merion, Haverford, and Radnor Townships, an area considered extreme wilderness with poor access to the city amenities. This disappointment did not dissipate easily and was renewed on several occasions when Penn's surveyors laid out parcels of lands to English settlers within the bounds of what the Welsh considered their Barony. This is certainly what is reflected in the complaints to the general assembly:

> in pretending to give them a town, and then by imposing unconscionable quit-rents, [the commissioners] make it worse by tenfold than a purchase would have been . . . and not only so, but the very land the town stands on, is not cleared of the Swedes' claims.

And we hope we need not be more express in charging thee; as thou tenders thy own honour and honesty, or the obligations thou art under to thy friends, and particularly thy first purchasers and adventurers in this province.[295]

These grievances were reiterated and referenced in reports during the year 1701, as well as on June 26, 1704, and June 10, 1707. There was no chance of sweeping these grievances under the rug. Year after year the courts discussed and debated. At issue was the secrecy with which the English commissioners operated in their land dealings. The petitioners complained "that the land in the liberties, actually surveyed for the good and benefit of the first purchasers, was designedly concealed from them." These individuals were not actually privy to the property to which they were gaining title. As it turns out, William Penn, through his commissioners, was over-promising acreage to both the original settlers and the incoming colonists. His successful promotions had caused him to oversell and overpromise the available land. Thus, the dealings were held in strict confidence to prevent participants from realizing they were being cheated. John Reed, the author of the abstract, notes, "those warrants were kept a profound secret; it was known but to a few there were such existing: so secret were they kept, that Mr. Lukens, the present surveyor-general, offered to lay the author a bett of one hundred pounds there were no such warrants: so positive was he, that he offered to have his arm cut off, in case such could be produced. After some altercations a bett was laid; which Mr. Lukens had the honour to, and generously did, pay."[296]

The fact that the Swanson brothers were promised 820 acres is stated in multiple documents. The bill that came to the assembly in 1701 was still being discussed in 1704. It is restated in Reed's 1774 abstract that "eight hundred and twenty acres of land were granted by the proprietors to Swanson and comp, in lieu of their right to the land where the city now stands."

William Penn's land exchange deed to the Swanson brothers was signed and dated in 1683. Yet thirteen years later, in 1696, according to the Recital of Deeds, when the brothers divided the Netopcom land equally among themselves, each brother took two hundred acres, solidly illustrating they received 220 acres less then they had been promised.[297]

The other thing that stands out from the assembly abstract Reed wrote is the statement that "the very land the town stands on, is not cleared of the Swedes' claims." Had the Swanson brothers attempted to fight Penn's land exchange proposal? Could they really have benefited from giving up their original lands, and what recourse would there have been if the brothers had simply wished to dismiss Penn's offer? An interesting account of the Swedish perspective comes from the journal of Pastor Per Kalm, a fellow Swede, written while he was visiting the colonies. Like Reed's abstract, Kalm's journal entry was written many years after Penn signed the actual land exchange deed—some sixty-five years later, on September 16, 1748:

> The town was built in the year 1683, or as others say in 1682, by the well-known Quaker William Penn, who got this whole province by a grant from Charles, the Second, King of England, after Sweden had given up claims to it. *** The place at that time was almost entirely a wilderness covered with thick forests, and belonged to three Swedish brothers called Svenssöner (sons of Sven) who had settled on it. They reluctantly left the place, the location of which was very advantageous. But at last they were persuaded

to leave it by Penn, who gave them, a few English miles from there, twice the space of land they had inhabited. However, Penn himself and his descendants after him have, by repeated insinuations, considerably lessened the ground belonging to the Swedes, under pretense that they have taken more than they should.[298]

Interestingly, John Reed's map of Philadelphia of 1774, drawn more than ninety years after the Swanson land exchange, clearly illustrates the Netopcom property and is labeled "Swan Swanson & Comp. 820 a. given in lieu of Land on which part of Philadelphia City now stands."[299]

Swan Swanson sold his two hundred acres to John Hood on July 22, 1696. That portion of the Netopcom property would then be renamed Hoodbury. On October 16, 1708, Hood deeded the land to his son Thomas. The description of the land contained in the Deed Book is very enlightening:

> [John Hood] assigns a Certain Tract of Land lyeing & being at NETOPCOM near Schoolkill in the County of Philadelphia and Province of Pensilvania With the Plantations and Buildings Now in the Possession . . . tract of Land Being One third part of Six hundred acres Granted by William Penn proprietor & Governor of the said Province soon after he became proprietor of the said Province and before the Cittye Philadelphia was seated thereon Unto Swan Swanson & others of the Inhabitants of Wiccoco In exchange for the Land where on the said Town of Philadelphia is now layd out & seated As by Warrant under his hand & Seal Dated the Third day of the sixth month Anno Domi 1683 to the Survey & Genrall for laying out—the same & Returned into the Secretary's Office the eleventh day of August 1685 By Virtue of the said Swan Swans & other.[300]

Perhaps William Lewis found it fortuitous that the land upon which he built his country villa was once owned by his wife Rosanna's Swedish ancestors—he purchased the property exactly one hundred years after her great-uncles had obtained the land from William Penn.

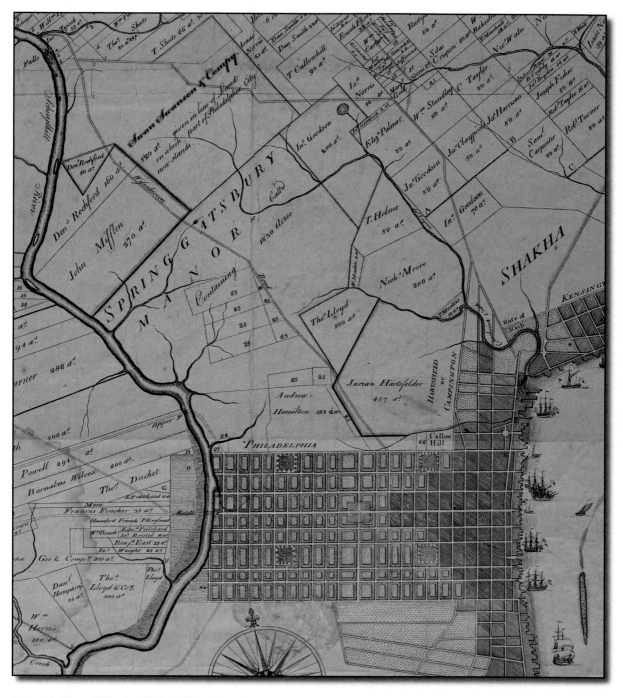

Map of the City and Liberties of Philadelphia, with the Catalogue of Purchasers, by John Reed, cartographer, engraved by James Smither, 1774. Note section featuring "Swan Swanson & Co." property in context to Penn's Philadelphia plan. Chew Family Papers, Historical Society of Pennsylvania.

Swanson property, detail of Map of the City of and Liberties of Philadelphia with the Catalogue of Purchasers, by John Reed, cartographer, engraved by James Smither, 1774. Chew Family Papers, Historical Society of Pennsylvania.

Sven Swensson
aka Swan Swanson
m.
Catharina Larsdotter

Gertrude Svensdotter
m. c1654
Jonas Nilsson

Olle Svensson
aka Woolly/Olle Swanson
m.
Lydia Ashman

Jonas Jonasson
aka Jonas Jones
m. 29 July 1702
Anne Seymour

Barbara Jones . . . . Barbara Jones
m. *2nd husband*   m. *1st husband*
30 March 1749   25 January 1742
John Lort   Samuel Crozier

Rosanna Lort   Margaret Crozier
m. 25 November 1771
Judge William Lewis

Sven Gunnarsson
(c1610-c1678)

Anders Svensson
aka Andrew/Anders Swanson
m.
Anna (___?___)

Daughter
name unknown
m.
Peter Mansson Lom

Credit Sandra Hewlett, Certified Genealogist

Suggested Further Reading

William Lewis and the History of Law in Philadelphia:

Robert R. Bell, *The Philadelphia Lawyer: A History*, 1735–1945 (Cranbury, NJ: Associated University Presses, 1992).

Horace Binney, *Leaders of the Old Bar of Philadelphia* (Philadelphia: C. Sherman & Son, 1859). Chapter on Lewis pp. 7–45.

> Binney's sketch of Lewis reprinted in the *Pennsylvania Magazine of History and Biography* 14, no. 1 (April 1890): 1–27.
>
> Also found in *Addresses Delivered March 13, 1902, and Papers Prepared or Republished to Commemorate The Centennial Celebration of the Law Association of Philadelphia, Pennsylvania, 1802–1902* (Philadelphia: Law Association of Philadelphia, 1906; repr. 1954), 87–106.

David Paul Brown, *The Forum; or Forty Years Full Practice at the Philadelphia Bar*, 2 vols. (Philadelphia: Robert H. Small, 1856). Chapter on Lewis pp. 444–62.

William Hamilton, comp., *Report of the Trial and Acquittal of Edward Shippen . . . and Jasper Yeates and Thomas Smith* (Lancaster: William Hamilton, 1805).

J. M. Hansen, *William Lewis: His Influences on Early American Law as a Philadelphia Lawyer, Republican*

Assemblyman, and Federalist Leader. Master's thesis, University of Northern Colorado, 1999.

"Letter of Peter S. DuPonceau to Thomas I. Wharton, Philadelphia, 3d June, 1837," in *Addresses Delivered March 13, 1902, and Papers Prepared or Republished to Commemorate the Centennial Celebration of the Law Association of Philadelphia, Pennsylvania* (Philadelphia: Law Association of Philadelphia, 1906), 265–77.

Maeva Marcus, editor, *The Documentary History of the Supreme Court of the United States, 1789–1800,* vol. 7, *Cases:* 1796–1797 (New York: Columbia University Press, 2003).

J. H. Martin, *Martin's Bench and Bar of Philadelphia* (Philadelphia: Rees Welsh, 1883).

Thomas R. Meehan, "Courts, Cases, and Counselors in Revolutionary and Post-Revolutionary Pennsylvania," *Pennsylvania Magazine of History and Biography* 91 (January 1967): 3–34.

"Memoirs of the late William Lewis, Esq. of the Philadelphia Bar" *Analectic Magazine* 1 (June 1820). ProQuest: American Periodicals Series Online. This publication used Primrose as its main source.

Philadelphia Bar Association: Recording the Proceedings, Addresses, and Historical Displays and Observances Incident to the commemoration of 150th Anniversary of the Association, 1802–1952 (Philadelphia: Buchanan, at the Sign of the Ivy Leaf, 1952).

Stephen B. Presser, *Studies in the History of the United States Courts of the Third Circuit, 1790–1980: A Bicentennial Project* (Washington: Government Printing Office, 1892).

William Primrose, "Biography of William Lewis" (written in 1820), *Pennsylvania Magazine of History and Biography* 20, no. 1 (April 1896): 30–40.

"*Respublica v. Abraham Carlisle,*" in Alexander J. Dallas, ed., *Report of Cases in the Supreme Court of Pennsylvania,* 4 vols. (Philadelphia, 1790–1807), 1:35.

G. S. Rowe, *Embattled Bench: The Pennsylvania Supreme Court and the Forging of a Democratic Society, 1684–1809* (Newark: University of Delaware Press, 1994).

Thomas J. Rueter, "William Lewis: First United States Attorney—Federal Courts 200," *Shingle* (Philadelphia Bar Association Quarterly Magazine) 52, no. 2 (Spring 1989).

The Supreme Court of the United States: Its Beginnings and Its Justices, 1790–1991 (Washington: Commission on the Bicentennial of the United States Constitution, reprinted by the Supreme Court Historical Society, 1992).

Erwin C. Surrency, "The Lawyer and the Revolution," *American Journal of Legal History* 8, no. 2 (April 1964): 125–35.

Henry J. Young, "Treason and its Punishment in Revolutionary Pennsylvania," *Pennsylvania Magazine of History and Biography* 90, no. 3 (July 1966): 287–313.

Abolition Movement:

Christopher Densmore, "Seeking Freedom in the Courts: The Work of the Pennsylvania Society for the Abolition of Slavery, and for the Relief of Free Negroes unlawfully held in Bondage, and for improving the condition of the African Race, 1775–1865," *Pennsylvania Legacies* 5, no. 2 (November 2005): 16–19.

Gary B. Nash and Jean R. Soderlund, *Freedom By Degrees: Emancipation in Pennsylvania and its Aftermath* (New York: Oxford University Press, 1991).

Richard S. Newman, "The Pennsylvania Abolition Society: Restoring a Group to Glory," *Pennsylvania Legacies* 5, no. 2 (November 2005): 6–10.

Phillip R. Seitz, "Tales from the Chew Family Papers: The Charity Castle Story," *Pennsylvania Magazine of History and Biography* 32, no. 1 (January 2008): 65–86.

Jean R. Soderlund, *Quakers and Slavery: A Divided Spirit* (Princeton: Princeton University Press, 1982).

David Waldstreicher, *Runaway America: Benjamin Franklin, Slavery, and the American Revolution* (New York: Hill and Wang, 2004).

Biographies and Writings of Persons of Interest:

H. W. Brands, *The First American: The Life and Times of Benjamin Franklin* (New York: Anchor Books, 2002).

James Thomas Flexner, *Washington: The Indispensible Man*, (New York: Little, Brown, 1969).

Paul L. Ford, ed., *The Works of Thomas Jefferson*, 12 vols. (New York: G. P. Putnam's Sons, 1904–1905). Thomas Jefferson's May 29, 1792, letter to George Hammond is found in volume 7.

James J. Kirschke, *Gouverneur Morris: Author, Statesman, and Man of the World* (New York: Thomas Dunne Books, 2005).

Mary-Jo Kline, ed., *Alexander Hamilton: A Biography in His Own Words* (New York: Newsweek, 1973. Distributed by Harper & Row).

David W. Maxey, *A Portrait of Elizabeth Willing Powel, 1743–1830* (Philadelphia: American Philosophical Society, 2006).

Dorothy Twohig, ed., *George Washington's Diaries: An Abridgement* (Charlottesville: University Press of Viriginia, 1999).

Carl Van Doren, *Benjamin Franklin*, 9th printing (New York: Viking, 1952).

Carl Van Doren, ed., *Benjamin Franklin's Autobiographical Writings*, 3rd printing (New York: Viking, 1952).

Raymond Walters, Jr., *Albert Gallatin: Jeffersonian Financier and Diplomat* (Pittsburgh: University of Pittsburgh Press, 1969).

Genealogy Resources:

Gilbert Cope, *Genealogy of the Sharpless Family* (Philadelphia: published for the family, 1887).

Gilbert Cope, *Genealogy of the Smedley Family* (Lancaster, PA: Wickersham Printing Co., 1901).

Peter Stebbins Craig and Kim-Eric Williams, eds., *Colonial Records of the Swedish Churches in Pennsylvania*, 5 vols. (Philadelphia: Swedish Colonial Society, 2006–09).

J. Smith Futhey and Gilbert Cope, *History of Chester County, Pennsylvania, with Genealogical and*

Biographical Sketches (Philadelphia: Louis H. Everts, 1881).

Hannah Benner Roach, *Colonial Philadelphians* (Philadelphia: Genealogical Society of Pennsylvania, 1999).

General Philadelphia History:

Susan Branson, *These Fiery Frenchified Dames: Women and Political Culture in Early National Philadelphia* (Philadelphia: University of Pennsylvania Press, 2001).

John Frederick Lewis, *The History of An Old Philadelphia Land Title: 208 South Fourth Street* (Philadelphia: Patterson and White, 1934).

Roger W. Moss, *Historic Houses of Philadelphia* (Philadelphia: University of Pennsylvania Press, 1998. A Barra Foundation Book). Section on Strawberry Mansion pp. 104–7.

Jacob Cox Parson, ed., *Extracts from the Diary of Jacob Hilzheimer, of Philadelphia, 1765–1798* (Philadelphia: Wm. F. Fell, 1893).

J. Thomas Scharf and Thompson Westcott, *History of Philadelphia, 1609–1884*, 3 vols. (Philadelphia: L. H. Everts, 1884).

John Fanning Watson, *Annals of Philadelphia, and Pennsylvania, in the Olden Time*, 3 vols. (Philadelphia; Edwin S. Stuart, 1905).

Russell F. Weigley et al., eds., *Philadelphia: A 300-Year History* (New York: W. W. Norton, 1892. A Barra Foundation Book).

George Bacon Wood and Frederick Dawson Stone, *Early History of the University of Pennsylvania, from its Origin to the Year 1827* (Philadelphia: J. B. Lippincott, 1896).

Politics:

Robert L. Brunhouse, *The Counter-Revolution in Pennsylvania, 1776–1790* (Harrisburg: Pennsylvania Historical and Museum Commission, 1942), especially pp. 10–52.

Merrill Jensen, ed., *The Documentary History of the Ratification of the Constitution, vol. 2, Ratification of the Constitution by the States: Pennsylvania* (Madison: State Historical Society of Wisconsin, 1976).

George David Rappaport, *Stability and Change in Revolutionary Pennsylvania: Banking, Politics, and Social Structure* (University Park: Pennsylvania State University Press, 1996).

G. S. Rowe, *Thomas McKean: The Shaping of an American Republicanism* (Boulder: Colorado Associated University Press, 1978).

Harry Marlin Tinkcom, *The Republicans and Federalists in Pennsylvania, 1790–1801: A Study in National Stimulus and Local Response* (Harrisburg: Pennsylvania Historical and Museum Commission, 1950).

Other Miscellaneous Resources:

Carrie Rebora Barratt and Ellen G. Miles, *Gilbert Stuart* (New York: Metropolitan Museum of Art / New Haven: Yale University Press, 2004). For Stuart in Philadelphia (1794–1803), see p. 129.

Hampton L. Carson, *A History of The Historical Society of Pennsylvania*, vol. 1 (Philadelphia: Historical Society of Pennsylvania, 1940).

Sally F. Griffith, *Serving History in a Changing World: The Historical Society of Pennsylvania in the Twentieth Century* (Philadelphia: Historical Society of Pennsylvania, 2001. Distributed by University of Pennsylvania Press).

Algot Mattsson, *New Sweden: The Dream of an Empire*, translated from the Swedish by Jan Teeland and Jeremy Franks (Gothenburg, Sweden: Tre Böcker Förlage, 1987).

Henry D. Paxson, *Where Pennsylvania History Began* (Philadelphia: George H. Buchanan, 1926).

Edgar P. Richardson, Brooke Hindle, and Lillian B. Miller, *Charles Willson Peale and his World* (New York: Harry N. Abrams, 1982. A Barra Foundation Book).

Ian W. Toll, *Six Frigates: The Epic History of the Foundation of the U.S. Navy* (New York: W. W. Norton, 2006).

Additional Documents Held at the Historical Society of Pennsylvania:

Appointment of William Lewis as Judge of the District Court of Pennsylvania, July 14, 1791 (copy), Historical Society of Pennsylvania Miscellaneous Collection.

William Bradford, Jr., to Elias Boudinot, January 10, 1790, Wallace MSS, Bradford Papers (for further background on the state constitution and direct election of state senators, an argument dominated by Lewis and Wilson as delegates of the State Constitutional Convention).

Journals of William Rawle, Sr., Rawle Family Papers.

William Lewis to General Otho H. Williams, Philadelphia, May 31, 1786, Dreer Collection 1:32–33.

Papers of Tench Coxe, Coxe Family Papers (for Lewis's speculation in western Pennsylvania).

Pennsylvania Abolition Society Papers.

Southwark Manuscript Map, 1789 (for Lewis's land holdings in Philadelphia).

Index

Endnotes

1   William E. Lingelback, "Carson Biographical Sketch," in Hampton L. Carson, *A History of The Historical Society of Pennsylvania*, vol. 1 (Philadelphia: Historical Society of Pennsylvania, 1940), ix.

2   Lingelback, "Biographical Sketch," x.

3   David Paul Brown, "William Lewis, L.L.D.," in *The Forum: or Forty Years Full Practice At the Philadelphia Bar*, vol. 1 (Philadelphia: R.H. Small, 1856), 455.

4   The words of Primrose, Binney, and Brown have made up the canon on the life and work of Judge William Lewis, and all have been referenced endlessly since their publication.

5   Thomas Allen Glenn, *Merion in the Welsh Tract* (Norristown, 1896; repr., Baltimore: Genealogical Publishing Company, 1970), 34.

6   Glenn, *Merion in the Welsh Tract*, 20.

7   Jane Levis Carter, *Edgmont: The Story of a Township* (Kennett Square, PA: Kennett Square Press, 1976), 106.

8   Lewis's birthdate was February 2 on the Julian Calendar, which was replaced in 1752.

9   "New England Women Plan Colonial House Tour," *Main Line Times*, May 10, 1977.

10   William Primrose, "Biography of William Lewis," *Pennsylvania Magazine of History and Biography* 20 (1896): 30.

11   "Letter of Peter S. DuPonceau to Thomas I. Wharton, Philadelphia, 3d June, 1837," in *The Law Association of Philadelphia: Addresses Delivered March 13, 1902, and Papers Prepared or Republished to Commemorate the Centennial Celebration of the Law Association of Philadelphia, Pennsylvania* (Philadelphia: Law Association of Philadelphia, 1906), 267. Hereafter cited as DuPonceau to Wharton.

12   DuPonceau to Wharton, 267.

13   Harold Donaldson Eberlein and Horace Mather Lippincott, *The Colonial Homes of Philadelphia and its Neighbourhood*, (Philadelphia: J. B. Lippincott, 1912), 59.

14   Brown, "William Lewis, L.L.D.," 447.

15   Whitfield J. Bell, Jr., *Patriot-Improvers: Biographical Sketches of Members of the American Philosophical Society*, vol. 1: 1743–1768 (Philadelphia: American Philosophical Society, 1997), 309.

16   Gerald J. St. John, "This is *Our* Bar," *Philadelphia Lawyer* 64, no. 4 (Winter 2002), http://www.philadelphiabar.org/page/TPLWinter02ThisIsOurBar.

17   Brown, "William Lewis, L.L.D.," 448.

[18] Horace Binney, "William Lewis," in *Leaders of the Old Bar of Philadelphia* (Philadelphia: C. Sherman & Son, 1859), 18.

[19] "Effective Supply Tax of the City of Philadelphia, 1781," *Pennsylvania Archives*, 3rd. ser., vol. 15 (Harrisburg, n.d.), 654, www.footnote.com, accessed June 27, 2011; John Lort Administration file no. 83 (1795), Philadelphia Register of Wills, Philadelphia City Hall; Philadelphia City Directory 1785 (Philadelphia: Francis White, 1785), 44, www.archive.org/details/philadelphiadire1785phil; Records of the Second Presbyterian Church, Philadelphia: Baptisms, Marriages and Burials, 1745-1833, in *Collections of the Genealogical Society of Pennsylvania*, 32 (Philadelphia 1898), 9-10. Joseph Lort was born May 27, 1756 and christened June 20, 1756.

[20] Church Records, St. Michael's and Zion Evangelical Lutheran Church, Marriages and Burials 1771–1784, p. 12, Collections of the Genealogical Society of Pennsylvania

[21] Bell, *Patriot-Improvers*, 309.

[22] Bell, *Patriot-Improvers*, 310.

[23] Primrose, "Biography of William Lewis," 32.

[24] Haverford College Library, Haverford, PA, Quaker Collection, Minutes of the Monthly Meeting of Friends of Philadelphia for the Southern District, 25 October 1775, p. TBD, (hereafter cited as Monthly Meeting Minutes).

[25] Monthly Meeting Minutes, 21 February 1776, p. 130.

[26] Monthly Meeting Minutes, 27 March 1776, p. 133.

[27] Primrose, "Biography of William Lewis," 32.

[28] John Fanning Watson, *Annals of Philadelphia, and Pennsylvania, in the Olden Time*, vol. 1 (Philadelphia: Edwin S. Stuart, 1905), 425.

[29] John Frederick Lewis, *The History of an Old Philadelphia Land Title: 208 South Fourth Street* (Philadelphia: Patterson and White Co., 1934), 112.

[30] Brown, "William Lewis, L.L.D.," 456.

[31] Brown, "William Lewis, L.L.D.," 455–56.

[32] Richard Green, "Chickasaws Visit President Washington (1794)," accessed at http://www.ushistory.org/presidentshouse/history/chickasaw.htm. Originally printed in *Chickasaw Times*, July 2009.

[33] Brown, "William Lewis, L.L.D.," 456.

[34] Robert L. Brunhouse, *The Counter-Revolution in Pennsylvania, 1776–1790* (Harrisburg: Pennsylvania Historical Commission, 1942), 33.

[35] Primrose, "Biography of William Lewis," 32–33.

[36] Binney, "William Lewis," 19.

[37] Jacob Cox Parsons, ed., *Extracts from the Diary of Jacob Hiltzheimer, of Philadelphia, 1765–1798* (Philadelphia: Wm F. Fell, 1893), 35.

[38] "Oaths taken before Dan Griffith," Manuscript 29560, Chester County Historical Society (West Chester, Pennsylvania).

[39] Robert L. Brunhouse, *The Counter-Revolution in Pennsylvania, 1776–1790*, 50.

[40] G. S. Rowe, *Thomas McKean: The Shaping of an American Republicanism* (Boulder: Colorado Associated University Press, 1978), 112.

[41] Henry J. Young, "Treason and its Punishment in Revolutionary Pennsylvania," *Pennsylvania Magazine of History and Biography* 90 (1966): 302.

[42] Rowe, *Thomas McKean*, 103.

[43] "Respublica v. Abraham Carlisle," in Alexander J. Dallas, ed., *Reports of cases ruled and adjudged in the several courts of the United States, and of Pennsylvania*, 4 vols. (Philadelphia: T. Bradford 1790–1807), 1:35.

[44] Rowe, *Thomas McKean*, 117.

[45] Thomas R. Meehan, "Courts, Cases, and Counselors in Revolutionary and Post-Revolutionary Pennsylvania," *Pennsylvania*

Magazine of History and Biography 91 (1967): 8, as quoted in G. S. Rowe, *Embattled Bench: The Pennsylvania Supreme Court and the Forging of a Democratic Society, 1684–1809* (Newark: University of Delaware Press, 1994), 143.

46 Binney, "William Lewis," 20–21.

47 Hampton L. Carson, "The Case of the Sloop 'Active,'" *Pennsylvania Magazine of History and Biography* 16 (1893): 385–86.

48 Rowe, *Thomas McKean*, 271.

49 Carson, "Sloop 'Active,'" 388–89.

50 Carson, "Sloop 'Active,'" 393.

51 Carson, "Sloop 'Active,'" 398.

52 Carson, "Sloop 'Active,'" 396.

53 Robert R. Bell, *The Philadelphia Lawyer: A History, 1735–1945* (Cranbury, NJ: Associated University Presses, 1992), 85.

54 Binney, "William Lewis," 24.

55 Rowe, *Thomas McKean*, 140–141.

56 "Respublica v. Joshua Buffington," in Dallas, *Reports*, 1:63.

57 Rowe, *Thomas McKean*, 139.

58 Cathy D. Matson and Wendy A. Woloson, *Risky Business: Winning and Losing in the Early American Economy, 1780–1850* (Philadelphia: Library Co. of Philadelphia, 2003), 3. Exhibition catalogue.

59 Morton J. Horwitz, *The Transformation of American Law, 1780–1860* (Cambridge: Harvard University Press, 1977), 253.

60 Raymond Walters, Jr., *Alexander James Dallas: Lawyer, Politician, Financier, 1759–1817* (Philadelphia: University of Pennsylvania Press, 1943), 101.

61 Brown, "William Lewis, L.L.D.," 452.

62 "Rivers v. Walker," in Dallas, *Reports*, 1:81.

63 "Hagner v. Musgrove," in Dallas, *Reports*, 1:82.

64 Rowe, *Thomas McKean*, 219–220.

65 Brown, "William Lewis, L.L.D.," 457.

66 Brown, "William Lewis, L.L.D.," 457.

67 Diary entries of July 16, 1782, and January 28, 1783, in *The Papers of Robert Morris*, ed. John Catanzariti, 9 vols. (Pittsburgh: University of Pittsburgh Press, 1973–2000), 5:558; 7:376.

68 Primrose, "Biography of William Lewis," 34.

69 Craig H. Horle, Joseph S. Foster, and Laurie M. Wolfe, eds., *Lawmaking and Legislators in Pennsylvania: A Biographical Dictionary*, vol. 3, 1757–1775 (University Park: Pennsylvania State University Press, 2005).

70 Gary Nash and Jean R. Soderlund, *Freedom By Degrees: Emancipation in Pennsylvania and Its Aftermath* (New York: Oxford University Press, 1991), 100–101.

71 Binney, "William Lewis," 25.

72 J. Thomas Scharf and Thompson Westcott, *History of Philadelphia, 1609–1884* (Philadelphia: L. H. Everts, 1884), 2:1528.

73 Nash and Soderlund, *Freedom By Degrees*, 101–102.

74 Nash and Soderlund, *Freedom By Degrees*, 115–23.

75 Edward Needles, *An Historical Memoir of the Pennsylvania Society, for Promoting the Abolition of Slavery; the Relief of Free Negroes Unlawfully Held in Bondage, and for Improving the Condition of the African Race,* (Philadelphia: Merrihew and Thompson, 1848), 27.

76 Constitution of the Pennsylvania Society for *Promoting the Abolition of Slavery, and the Relief of Free Negroes, Unlawfully*

Held in Bondage; enlarged at Philadelphia, April 23, 1787. William Lewis's personal copy from the family papers.

77 Richard S. Newman, "The Pennsylvania Abolition Society: Restoring a Group to Glory," *Pennsylvania Legacies* 5, no. 2 (2005): 7.

78 William Rawle, Address of the Pennsylvania Abolition Society," April 29, 1819, Rawle Family Papers, Historical Society of Pennsylvania, Philadelphia.

79 Richard S. Newman, "The Pennsylvania Abolition Society."

80 Tench Coxe to David Barclay, March 6, 1787, Pennsylvania Abolition Society Papers, Historical Society of Pennsylvania, Philadelphia (hereafter PAS Papers, HSP), microfilm reel 15.

81 Christopher Densmore, "Seeking Freedom in the Courts: The Work of the Pennsylvania Society for promoting the Abolition of Slavery, and for the Relief of Free Negroes unlawfully held in Bondage, and for improving the condition of the African Race, 1775–1865," *Pennsylvania Legacies* 5, no. 2 (2005): 18.

82 Densmore, "Seeking Freedom in the Courts," 18.

83 "Respublica v. Negro Betsey, et al.," in Dallas, *Reports*, 1:469.

84 "Respublica v. Gaoler of Philadelphia County," in Jasper Yeates, ed., *Report of Cases Adjudged in the Supreme Court of Pennsylvania*, vol. 1 (St. Louis, 1871): 368.

85 *An Act to Explain and Amend an Act, entitled, "An Act for the Gradual Abolition of Slavery"* (Philadelphia: T. Bradford, 1788).

86 Parsons, *Diary of Jacob Hiltzheimer*, 144.

87 *In re* Slave Kitty, Philadelphia, 1793, Documents concerning court cases in which slaves were awarded freedom, 1773–1883, PAS Papers, HSP, microfilm reel 25.

88 "Commonwealth v. Chambre," in Dallas, *Reports*, 4:143–44.

89 Rowe, *Embattled Bench*, 221.

90 Phillip R. Seitz, "Tales from the Chew Family Papers: The Charity Castle Story," *Pennsylvania Magazine of History and Biography*, 132 (2008): 68.

91 Seitz, "The Charity Castle Story," 68.

92 Seitz, "The Charity Castle Story," 76.

93 Seitz, "The Charity Castle Story," 81.

94 Seitz, "The Charity Castle Story," 83.

95 Lewis estate papers.

96 Primrose, "Biography of William Lewis," 34–35.

97 Rowe, *Thomas McKean*, 243; see also Thomas McKean papers, Historical Society of Pennsylvania.

98 Robert L. Brunhouse, *The Counter-Revolution in Pennsylvania, 1776–1790* (Harrisburg: Pennsylvania Historical Commission, 1942), 206.

99 Rowe, *Thomas McKean*, 243.

100 Brunhouse, *Counter-Revolution*, 206.

101 Rowe, *Thomas McKean*, 245.

102 Rowe, *Thomas McKean*, 249.

103 Rowe, *Thomas McKean*, 252.

104 *Independent Gazetteer* (Philadelphia), July 11, 1788.

105 Rowe, *Embattled Bench*, 195.

106 "Respublica v. Oswald," in Dallas, *Reports*, 1:319.

107 Rowe, *Thomas McKean*, 253.

108 Rowe, *Thomas McKean*, 256.

[109] Rowe, *Thomas McKean*, 256; see also Atlee MSS, Library Company of Philadelphia, Philadelphia.

[110] Harry Marlin Tinkcom, *The Republicans and Federalists in Pennsylvania, 1790–1801: A Study in National Stimulus and Local Response* (Harrisburg: Pennsylvania Historical and Museum Commission, 1950), 8.

[111] Tinkcom, *Republicans and Federalists in Philadelphia*, 9.

[112] Lewis estate papers.

[113] George Bacon Wood and Frederick Dawson Stone, *Early History of the University of Pennsylvania from its Origin to the Year 1827*, 3rd ed. (Philadelphia: J. B. Lippincott, 1896), 99.

[114] James R. Perry and James M. Buchanan, "Admission to the Supreme Court Bar, 1790–1800: A Case Study of Institutional Change," in William F. Swindler, ed., *Yearbook 1983* (Washington, D.C.: Supreme Court Historical Society, 1983), 11. "Counselor" was the designation for those who could plead cases before the court, while anyone admitted as an "attorney" would only be allowed to prepare documents.

[115] Perry and Buchanan, "Admission to the Supreme Court Bar," 15.

[116] Jason S. Lantzer, Esther McFarland, and Garth C. Herrick, *Portrait Symposium on the Life of the Honorable William Lewis, First United States Attorney and Second Judge of the District of Pennsylvania* (Philadelphia, 2010).

[117] Don Reilly, Norman Murphy, and Chuck Timanus, eds., *The Supreme Court of the United States: Its Beginnings and Its Justices, 1790–1991* (Washington, D.C.: Supreme Court Historical Society, 1992), 243–44.

[118] Lewis to George Washington, July 8, 1791, in Lewis estate papers.

[119] Lewis estate papers.

[120] Lewis estate papers.

[121] Lewis to Thomas Jefferson, July 17, 1791, in Lewis estate papers.

[122] Journals of William Rawle, Sr., Rawle Family Papers, Historical Society of Pennsylvania.

[123] James Thomas Flexner, *Washington: The Indispensible Man* (Boston: Little, Brown and Company, 1969), 240.

[124] Binney, "William Lewis," 26–27.

[125] Theodore W. Bean, *History of Montgomery County, Pennsylvania* (Philadelphia: Everts & Peck, 1884), 534.

[126] Flexner, Washington, 241.

[127] Binney, "William Lewis," 28.

[128] Binney, "William Lewis," 29.

[129] Thomas Jefferson to Lewis, March 31, 1791, Lewis estate papers.

[130] Thomas Jefferson to Lewis, April 5, 1791, Lewis estate papers.

[131] Rowe, *Thomas McKean*, 267.

[132] Tinkcom, *Republicans and Federalists in Philadelphia*, 52.

[133] Tinkcom, *Republicans and Federalists in Philadelphia*, 54.

[134] Tinckom, *Republicans and Federalists in Philadelphia*, 55.

[135] Tinkcom, *Republicans and Federalists in Philadelphia*, 56.

[136] Tinkcom, *Republicans and Federalists in Philadelphia*, 58.

[137] Tinkcom, *Republicans and Federalists in Philadelphia*, 60.

[138] William Lewis to Editor, *Federal Gazette*, October 9, 1792.

[139] Roland M. Baumann, "John Swanwick: Spokesman for 'Merchant-Republicanism' in Philadelphia, 1790–1798," *Pennsylvania Magazine of History and Biography* 97 (1973): 148–49.

[140] Baumann, "John Swanwick," 147.

[141] *Federal Gazette*, October 9, 1792.

[142] Baumann, "John Swanwick," 149.

143 Binney, "William Lewis," 29–30.

144 Binney, "William Lewis," 29.

145 Raymond Walters, Jr., *Albert Gallatin, Jeffersonian Financier and Diplomat* (Pittsburgh: University of Pittsburgh Press, 1969), 59.

146 Russell F. Weigley et al., Philadelphia: A 300-Year History (New York: W.W. Norton, 1982; a Barra Foundation book), 202.

147 "Thomas Jefferson," White House website, www.whitehouse.gov/about/presidents/thomasjefferson.

148 William Lewis, "To the Federal Electors of Pennsylvania," United States' *Gazette*, September 21, 1805.

149 Journals of William Rawle, Sr., Rawle Family Papers, Historical Society of Pennsylvania.

150 Edgar Preston Richardson, Brooke Hindle, and Lillian B. Miller, *Charles Willson Peale and His World* (New York, H. N. Abrams, 1983), 68.

151 Richardson, Hindle, and Miller, *Peale and His World*, 185–86.

152 *Columbian Magazine*, or *Monthly Miscellany*, May 1789.

153 Journals of William Rawle, Sr., Rawle Family Papers, Historical Society of Pennsylvania.

154 For further information, see Epilogue, section II, "The Land Title History of Summerville."

155 Rolls of the Carpenters Company in Philadelphia, 1773–1794, www.ushistory.org/carpentershall/company/allmembers.asp

156 William Lewis to Mrs. Livingston (Philadelphia, n.d.), Historic Strawberry Mansion exhibit.

157 Craig Morrison, Architect, "A Historic Structure Report for Strawberry Mansion, East Fairmount Park, Philadelphia, PA," January 1986, Fairmount Park Archives, Philadelphia.

158 John C. Poppelier, S. Allen Chambers, Jr., and Nancy B. Schwartz, Historic American Buildings Survey, *What Style Is It? A Guide to American Architecture* (Hoboken, NJ: John Wiley & Sons, 1983), 30.

159 Roger W. Moss, *Historic Houses of Philadelphia* (Philadelphia: University of Pennsylvania Press, 1998; a Barra Foundation book), 104–7.

160 Morrison, "Historic Structure Report for Strawberry Mansion."

161 Matthew Carey, *A Short Account of the Malignant Fever, Lately Prevalent in Philadelphia* (Philadelphia: Printed by the Author, 1794), 10.

162 Benjamin Rush, *Observations Upon the Origin of the Malignant Bilious, or Yellow Fever in Philadelphia, and Upon the Means of Preventing It: Addressed to the Citizens of Philadelphia (Philadelphia: Budd and Bartram, 1799).*

163 Carey, *Account of the Malignant Fever*, 16.

164 Henry D. Biddle, ed., Extracts from the Journal of Elizabeth Drinker (Philadelphia: J. B. Lippincott, 1889), 189.

165 Lewis, *History of an Old Philadelphia Land Title*, 111.

166 Carey, *Account of the Malignant Fever*, 24.

167 Jim Murphy, *An American Plague: The True and Terrifying Story of the Yellow Fever Epidemic of 1793* (New York: Clarion Books, 2003).

168 Carey, *Account of the Malignant Fever*, 46.

169 Rush, *Observations Upon the Origin*, 203.

170 Bob Arnebeck, *Destroying Angel: Benjamin Rush, Yellow Fever, and the Birth of Modern Medicine* (online novel), http://bobarnebeck.com/fever1793.html.

171 *Pennsylvania Gazette*, December 18, 1799.

172 Susan Branson, *These Fiery Frenchified Dames: Women and Political Culture in Early National Philadelphia* (Philadelphia: University of Pennsylvania Press, 2001), 103, 104.

173 Weigel et al., *Philadelphia: A 300-Year History*, 191. Many of Peale's patriot portraits are presently on view at the Second

Bank on Chestnut Street in the Independence National Historic Park.

174 Carrie Rebora Barratt and Ellen G. Miles, *Gilbert Stuart* (New York: Metropolitan Museum of Art / New Haven: Yale University Press, 2004), 129.

175 The Washington portrait was later given to Lewis's son Josiah. It is believed that Josiah gave it to a friend who later sold it. Stuart's portrait of Lewis remained in the possession of his second wife, Frances Durdin Lewis, until her death, when it was bequeathed to William's grandson, also named William Lewis. The portrait remains in family hands to this day. In addition, Stuart's pupil John Neagle painted an early copy of the portrait; it now hangs in the Law Library of the Philadelphia Bar Association. The family granted permission for a second copy based on the original, which hangs today at Strawberry Mansion. The Strawberry Mansion copy was painted by Nicholas Cortiglia in the early 1950s. Two additional copies of the Stuart portrait were permitted in 2007, based on access to the original, and painted by Garth C. Herrick, a graduate of the Pennsylvania Academy of Fine Arts. The first Herrick copy was done at the request of the Historical Society of the United States District Court in honor of Lewis's work as the First United States Attorney and Second Judge of the District of Pennsylvania. It is displayed in the ceremonial courtroom at the United States Courthouse at Sixth and Market Streets in Philadelphia. The second Herrick copy was painted for the McFarland family.

176 Frank H. Goodyear, Jr., "A History of the Pennsylvania Academy of the Fine Arts, 1805–1976," in *In This Academy: The Pennsylvanian Academy of the Fine Arts 1805–1976* (Philadelphia: Pennsylvania Academy of Fine Arts, 1976). Exhibition catalogue.

177 Francis Durdin Lewis, William's second wife, provided special instructions to Lewis's grandson in her will regarding the Stuart portrait of her husband. She wrote that she hoped "he will not part with it, but keep it through his life or give it to the academy of Fine Arts in Philadelphia as it is an excellent likeness." While Lewis's grandson chose to keep that portrait in the family, other Stuart portraits became early gifts to the institution. Of note are two of his portraits from the Willing family sisters, Elizabeth Willing Jackson and Abigail Willing Peters.

178 Bell, *The Philadelphia Lawyer*, 99; Scharf and Westcott, History of Philadelphia, 2:1,555.

179 James L. Whitehead, ed., "The Autobiography of Peter Stephen Du Ponceau," *Pennsylvania Magazine of History and Biography* 63 (1939): 189–91, 215, 260; Jennifer D. Henderson, "'A Blaze of Recognition and the Echo of a Name': The Legal Career of Peter Stephen DuPonceau in Post Revolutionary Philadelphia" (MA Thesis: Florida State University, 2004): 9, 12-16; *Addresses Delivered March 13, 1902 and Papers Prepared or Republished to Commemorate the Centennial Celebration of the Law Association of Philadelphia, 1802-1902,* (Philadelphia, 1902) 267-70.

180 Daniel Agnew, *Address to the Allegheny County Bar Association* (Pittsburgh, 1889), 33–34.

181 *Albany Gazette*, December 29, 1820.

182 J. H. Powell, *Richard Rush: Republican Diplomat, 1780–1859* (Philadelphia: University of Pennsylvania Press, 1942).

183 Carson, *History of The Historical Society of Pennsylvania*, 1:208; Thomas Payne Goven, *Nicholas Biddle. Nationalist and Public Banker, 1786–1844* (Chicago: University of Chicago Press, 1959), 1–12, 19–27.

184 *North American*, February 28, 1844.

185 Stephen Agard and Margaret Lewis marriage, August 9, 1792, Marriage Records of the Swedes' Church (Gloria Dei), 1750–1810, in John B. Linn and W. H. Egle, eds., *Pennsylvania Archives*, ser. 2, vol. 8, *Record of Pennsylvania Marriages Prior to 1810* (Harrisburg: Clarence M. Busch, 1896), 301. Accessed at http://usgwarchives.net/pa/1pa/paarchivesseries/series2/vol8/pass810.html.

186 Gilbert Cope, *Genealogy of the Smedley Family* (Lancaster, PA: Wickersham Printing Company, 1901); "Lists of Students in the College, 1790–1799," in Mary D. McConaghy, Michael Silberman, and Irina Kalashnikova, *Penn in the 18th Century* online exhibit, University of Pennsylvania University Archives and Records Center, www.archives.upenn.edu/histy/features/1700s/students1790s.html.

187 *Claypoole's Daily Advertiser*, March 5, 1799.

188 K–Mc Surnames, Marriage Record of Christ Church, Philadelphia,1709–1806, in *Pennsylvania Archives*, ser. 2, 8:164. Accessed at http://www.usgwarchives.net/pa/1pa/paarchivesseries/series2/vol8/pass85.html.

189 Cope, *Genealogy of the Smedley Family*, 781, no. 2495.

[190] Marriage Record of Christ Church, *Pennsylvania Archives*, ser. 2, 8:164.

[191] Frances Lewis bible, Frances Durdin Lewis papers, Western Reserve Historical Society, Cleveland, Ohio.

[192] *Dunlap's American Daily Advertiser*, June, 14, 1793; Lewis family papers; Frances Durdin Lewis papers, Western Reserve Historical Society.

[193] William Lewis to Josiah Lewis (Wilkes-Barre, PA), January 18, 1810, Lewis family papers.

[194] Cope, *Genealogy of the Smedley Family*, 781, no. 2495.

[195] The couple survived well enough without their family resources until George's father, near the end of his life, relinquished his threat. Louisa Agard did eventually marry Samuel Green, although she did not do so until after the death of her grandfather. William Rawle refers to her as "Louisa Agard" in a handwritten note dated April 24, 1820, on a document she had given him. However, a letter dated November 24, 1820, was written to William Rawle from Louisa Green, Edgmont. It appears she married Samuel sometime in those intervening seven months.

[196] Walters, *Alexander James Dallas*, 101.

[197] Rowe, *Embattled Bench*, 205.

[198] Rowe, *Embattled Bench*, 209.

[199] "Respublica v. Keppele," in Yeates, *Report*, 1:234.

[200] "Respublica v. Keppele," in Yeates, *Report*, 1:235.

[201] Rowe, *Embattled Bench*, 210.

[202] "Georgia v. Brailsford," in Dallas, *Reports*, 3:1.

[203] Maeva Marcus, "Georgia v. Brailsford," *Journal of Supreme Court History* 21, no. 2 (1996): 58.

[204] Marcus, "Georgia v. Brailsford," 62.

[205] Marcus, "Georgia v. Brailsford," 67.

[206] Sequestered John Nicholson papers, 1765–1852, Manuscript Group 96, Pennsylvania Historical and Museum Commission (PHMC), Harrisburg.

[207] Parson, ed., *Hiltzheimer Diary*, 202–4.

[208] John Nicholson papers, PHMC.

[209] "Ware, Administrator of Jones v. Hylton, et al.," in Dallas, *Reports*, 1:199.

[210] Maeva Marcus, ed., *Documentary History of the Supreme Court, 1789–1800*, vol. 7, Cases: 1796–1797 (New York: Columbia University Press, 2003), 320. Emphasis in original.

[211] Jean M. Hansen, *William Lewis: His Influences on Early American Law as a Lawyer, Republican Assemblyman, and Federalist Leader* (master's thesis, University of Colorado, 1999), 104.

[212] Jean Smith, "Tribute to John Marshall on the 250th Anniversary of His Birth," excerpted speech in *Supreme Court Historical Society Quarterly* 26, no. 3 (2005): 6.

[213] Rowe, *Embattled Bench*, 214–14.

[214] Ian W. Toll, *Six Frigates: The Epic History of the Foundation of the U.S. Navy* (New York: W.W Norton, 2006), 39.

[215] Alexander Hamilton, Federalist Papers, no. 11, November 24, 1787.

[216] David L. Sloss, "Judicial Foreign Policy: Lessons from the 1790s" (June 2008), Social Science Research Network, http://ssrn.com/abstract=1144060.

[217] Sloss, "Judicial Foreign Policy."

[218] Sloss, "Judicial Foreign Policy."

[219] Hansen, *William Lewis* thesis, 105.

[220] "Talbot v. Janson," in Dallas, *Reports*, 3:133.

[221] "Talbot v. Janson," in Dallas, *Reports*, 3:150.

[222] "Talbot v. Janson," in Dallas, *Reports*, 3:153.

223 "Talbot v. Janson," in Dallas, *Reports*, 3:153.

224 Sloss, "Judicial Foreign Policy."

225 Toll, *Six Frigates*, 43.

226 Thomas P. Slaughter, *The Whiskey Rebellion: Frontier Epilogue to the American Revolution* (New York: Oxford University Press, 1986), 218–19.

227 Thomas Jefferson to James Madison, December 28, 1794, in Merrill D. Peterson, ed., *Thomas Jefferson: Writings* (New York: Viking Press, 1984), 1,015–17.

228 Hansen, *William Lewis*, 46.

229 "United States v. The Insurgents of Pennsylvania," in Dallas, *Reports*, 2:335.

230 Jane Shaffer Elsmere, "The Trials of John Fries," *Pennsylvania Magazine of History and Biography* 103 (1979): 437; Walters, *Alexander James Dallas*, 80–81.

231 Elsmere, "Trials of John Fries," 438.

232 Lewis to Hamilton, October 11, 1800, in Harold C. Syrett, *Papers of Alexander Hamilton*, 26 vols. (New York: Columbia University Press, 1977), 25:153.

233 Elsmere, "Trials of John Fries," 443, 444.

234 Du Ponceau to Wharton, 273.

235 Maeva Marcus, "George Washington's Appointments to the Supreme Court," *Journal of Supreme Court History* 24, no. 3 (1999): 243 54.

236 Stephen B. Presser, *Studies in the History of the United States Courts of the Third Circuit, 1790–1980: A Bicentennial Project* (Washington: Government Printing Office, 1892), 244.

237 Binney, "William Lewis," 41–42, 103–4.

238 Journals of William Rawle, Sr., Rawle Family Papers, Historical Society of Pennsylvania.

239 Du Ponceau to Wharton, 271–75.

240 Miller Center, University of Virginia, "Thomas Jefferson: Domestic Affairs," American President Online Reference Resource, http://millercenter.org/academic/americanpresident/jefferson/essays/biography/4.

241 *Connecticut Centinel*, February 23, 1802, Emphasis mine.

242 Chief Justice Warren Burger, "Mr. Jefferson, Mr. Marshall, Mr. Burr, and Murphy's Law" (keynote speech, National Society of Colonial Dames of America, Mayflower Hotel, Washington DC, October 27, 1980).

243 Burger, "Jefferson, Marshall, Burr, and Murphy's Law."

244 Peter Du Ponceau to Wharton, "Letter to Thomas I. Wharton," 266.

245 Brown, "William Lewis, L.L.D.," 561–62.

246 *American Daily Advertiser*, August 2, 1804.

247 *Charleston Courier*, August 17, 1807.

248 Brown, "William Lewis, L.L.D.," 451.

249 Binney, "William Lewis," 43.

250 Brown, "William Lewis, L.L.D.," 451.

251 Binney, "William Lewis," 44, 105.

252 *Poulson's American Daily Advertiser*, August 17, 1819.

253 Lewis estate papers.

254 Christ Church and St. Peter's Burials 1782–1900 and Mr. Cummins Private Register 1726–1741 (Collections of the Genealogical Society of Pennsylvania, 1907), no.176, 3747.

255 *The Franklin Gazette*, August 20, 1819.

256   Here Jackson quotes from Job 29:11–13.

257   William Jackson, "Obituary of William Lewis," *Poulson's American Daily Advertiser*, August 19, 1819.

258   William Jackson, "Obituary of William Lewis," *Poulson's American Daily Advertiser*, August 20, 1819, in Lewis family papers.

259   *Poulson's American Daily Advertiser*, August 31, 1819.

260   Philadelphia City Archives, Deed Book A M, No. 25, p. 660, June 1, 1832.

261   Lewis family papers. See also papers of Tench Coxe in the Coxe Family Papers, Historical Society of Pennsylvania.

262   Report of Auditor, Estate of William Lewis, filed July 16, 1835, Philadelphia Orphans' Court Records, accessed Philadelphia City Hall, March 18, 1972.

263   Report of Auditor, Estate of William Lewis.

264   Lewis family papers.

265   Indigent Widows' and Single Women's Society/Ralston House Records, Historical Society of Pennsylvania.

266   Lewis family papers.

267   All remaining references in this section may be found in "Title Papers, Fairmount Park Property," Box 3A, "George Crock, grantor" file, Philadelphia City Archives.

268   *Poulson's American Daily Advertiser*, June 21, 1810, and April 15, 1813.

269   *Pennsylvania Packet*, January 24, 1774.

270   Mary Anne Hines, Gordon Marshall, and William Woys Weaver, *The Larder Invaded: Reflections on Three Centuries of Philadelphia Food and Drink* (Philadelphia: Library Company of Philadelphia, 1987; Historical Society of Pennsylvania, 1987), 57; James A. Beard, "Philly the Ice Cream Capital," *Los Angeles Times*, August 5, 1971, J4; Scharf and Westcott, *History of Philadelphia*, 945.

271   Strawberry Mansion brochure, 3rd ed. (December 1946), in the author's personal collection.

272   Morrison, "Historic Structure Report for Strawberry Mansion."

273   *Public Ledger*, July 22, 1848.

274   *Philadelphia Inquirer,* December 17, 1869.

275   Jay Platt "Strawberry Mansion: The History of a Schuylkill River Villa" (a report compiled for University of Pennsylvania Professor Roger W. Moss, 1994).

276   Ben M. Vorpahl, "Henry James and Owen Wister," *Pennylvania Magazine of History and Biography* 95 (1971): 294.

277   Strawberry Mansion brochure, 3rd ed. (December 1946), in the author's personal collection.

278   Henry D. Paxon, *Sketch and Map of a Trip from Philadelphia to Tinicum Island, Delaware County, Pennsylvania . . .* (Philadelphia: George H. Buchanan, 1926), 15.

279   Paxon, *Sketch and Map*, 15.

280   William J. Buck, *History of Montgomery County within The Schuylkill Valley* (Norristown: E.L. Acker, 1856), 10.

281   Paxon, *Sketch and Map*, 19.

282   Paxon, *Sketch and Map*, 21.

283   Paxon, *Sketch and Map*, 26.

284   Swedish Colonial Society website, www.colonialswedes.org; see also Peter S. Craig, "Jonas Nilsson in the News 315 Years after his Death," *Swedish Colonial News* 3, no. 8 (Spring 2008).

285   Swedish Colonial Society website.

286   Swedish Colonial Society website.

287   Paxon, *Sketch and Map*, 31.

288   Swedish Colonial Society website.

289 Paxon, *Sketch and Map*, 31.

290 Weigley et al., *Philadelphia: A 300-Year History*.

291 William Henry Egle, ed., *Pennsylvania Archives*, ser. 3, vol. 3, *Old Rights, Proprietary Rights, Virginia Entries, and Soldiers Entitled to Donation Lands, with an Explanation of Reed's Map of Philadelphia* (Harrisburg: Clarence Busch, 1896).

292 John McIlhenny, "On the Dating of Strawberry Mansion," *Fairmount Park Historical Quarterly* 1, no 2 (March 1984).

293 John Reed, "An Explanation of the Map of Philadelphia" in Pennsylvania Archives, 3rd. ser., 3:318.

294 Glenn, *Merion in the Welsh Tract*, 21.

295 Reed, "Explanation of the Map," in *Pennsylvania Archives*, 3rd. ser., 3:318.

296 Reed, "Explanation of the Map," in *Pennsylvania Archives*, 3rd ser., 3:323.

297 Deed between William Penn and the Swanson brothers (1683), Philadelphia City Archives; Strawberry Mansion Files, chain of title. Fairmount Park Commission, Office of the Park Historian, Philadelphia, Pennsylvania.

298 Peter S. Craig and Kim-Eric Williams, eds., *Colonial Records of the Swedish Churches of Pennsylvania*, vol. 4, *From Lidman to Nilsman, 1719 1750* (Philadelphia: Swedish Colonial Society, Philadelphia 2008), 259.

299 "Map of the City of Liberties of Philadelphia, With the Catalogue of Purchasers . . . ," by John Reed, cartographer (1774), engraved by James Smither, Chew Family Papers, Historical Society of Pennsylvania.

300 Deed of John Hood to his Son Thomas, October 16, 1708, Philadelphia City Archives, Deed Book H, No 7, pp. 119–21.